DATE DUE

WITHDRAWN

Style Manuals of the English-Speaking World: A Guide

by John Bruce Howell

 ORYX PRESS
1983

The rare Arabian Oryx is believed to have inspired the myth of the unicorn. This desert antelope became virtually extinct in the early 1960s. At that time several groups of international conservationists arranged to have 9 animals sent to the Phoenix Zoo to be the nucleus of a captive breeding herd. Today the Oryx population is over 400 and herds have been returned to reserves in Israel, Jordan, and Oman.

Copyright © 1983 by
The Oryx Press
2214 North Central at Encanto
Phoenix, Arizona 85004

Published simultaneously in Canada

Printed and Bound in the United States of America

Library of Congress Cataloging in Publication Data Ref.
PN
147
Howell, John Bruce, 1941–   H68
    Style manuals of the English-speaking world.   1983

    Includes index.
    1. Authorship—Style manuals—Bibliography.
I. Title.
Z5165.H68   1983   [PN147]   016.808'02   82-42916
ISBN 0-89774-089-0

Contents

Foreword

In 1953, the Association of College and Research (formerly Reference) Libraries published Mary R. Kinney's *Bibliographical Style Manuals: A Guide to Their Use in Documentation and Research,* which listed style requirements for both books and journals in the humanities, the social sciences, and the sciences. As the title indicates, Professor Kinney searched out bibliographic styles as advocated in manuals or by organizations. While much of her work is now of historical interest only, her method was a good one and has been adopted in the present work with the exception of style manuals in and for individual periodicals, which have been omitted because of their large number. However, guides to the style of journals are included.

Two other guides to style manuals deserve mention. In 1971, the Reference Department of McGill University Library (Montreal) issued *A Student's Guide to Style Manuals* (not further updated), which lists 19 titles. The other is *Style Guides for Technical Reports, Journal Articles, Dissertations, Term Papers, Publications [and] Theses* prepared by the library staff and issued by the Librarian's Office of the University of California (Santa Barbara) in 1975; the latest revision, 1981, has 127 entries and is particularly useful for its annotations.

Acknowledgments

The compiler wishes to thank the following researchers, scholars, and librarians who provided both information and guidance in the preparation of this guide: D. W. Krummel, Lawrence W. S. Auld, Kathryn Luther Henderson, Walter Coleman Allen, and Yvette Scheven, all faculty of the Graduate School of Library and Information Science, University of Illinois at Urbana-Champaign, Urbana, IL. Especially helpful was the staff of the Illinois Research and Reference Center, The Library, University of Illinois at Urbana-Champaign, Urbana, IL, who obtained many of the style manuals in this guide on interlibrary loan from other North American libraries.

Ruth S. Freitag and Joanne M. Zellers, Library of Congress, provided the compiler with many citations from Library of Congress cards and computer data files in the initial stages of preparation of the guide. Barbara M. Howell proofread the final version and provided editorial support and inspiration.

Introduction

This is a guide to style manuals and author's guides from the English-language publishing communities of Australia, Canada, India, New Zealand, Nigeria, Pakistan, Papua New Guinea, the Philippines, the United Kingdom, the United States, and Zimbabwe.

SCOPE

Criteria for Inclusion

Three criteria have been used to accept or reject a manual. First, the manual must be current, that is, published between 1970 and 1983. However, older manuals are included if they contain a presentation of style elements that has not been superseded. In most cases, these older manuals are "classics" and are well respected. Second, the style manual must be at least 5 pages long. This criterion permits including most author's guides, frequently short statements of house style written especially for new authors to acquaint them with the particulars of a publisher's requirements. In many cases, the author is sent to one or more of the major style manuals for more explanation of publishing problems. Third, the manual must be in English.[1]

The style used by any particular journal is generally found either in the pages of that journal or is obtained by writing to the editors. Within the last decade, many different publishing houses began to publish directories to all aspects of journals in a particular field. These directories always include indications of the style used by the journals listed. Because they include "journal style," they are listed separately in this guide following style manuals which are termed "general style."

---

[1]A multilingual bibliography of style manuals is the United Nations Educational, Scientific, and Cultural Organization, *Bibliography of Publications Designed to Raise the Standard of Scientific Literature* ([Paris: 1963]), which lists 359 entries in English, French, Russian, Spanish, German, Bulgarian, Danish, Polish, and Czech.

Criteria for Exclusion

GUIDES AND GRAMMARS FOR WRITING ENGLISH

Many books in print use the terms "style" and "manual." Frequently, the usage of "style manual" is confusing for authors, editors, and students who cannot determine the contents without examining the book. Often the book turns out to be a guide to writing better English. Guides and manuals devoted to prescriptive English grammar and thesauri are excluded from this guide.[2]

TECHNICAL WRITING

Technical writing includes style manuals on writing not only for government and industry, but also for business and science. Bibliographic coverage for the former is excellent and these titles have been excluded from this guide.[3] The literature of the latter is not well known and is obscured in the large bibliographies of technical writing. For this reason, style manuals for business, science, and the individual sciences are included within the scope of this guide.

UNIVERSITY STYLE GUIDES

Many universities issue style manuals for their own students at both the undergraduate and the graduate level. With the exception of style manuals of university presses (*see* pp. 50–61), style guides of individual universities and their faculties are excluded from this guide.

---

[2]A current list of style manuals for the improvement of written English is in the Modern Language Association of America, *MLA Handbook for Writers of Research Papers, Theses, and Dissertations* (New York: Modern Language Association of America, 1977), pp. 7–8.

[3]Three current bibliographies on technical writing are Gerald J. Alred, Diana C. Reep, and Mohan R. Limaye, *Business and Technical Writing: An Annotated Bibliography of Books, 1880-1980.* (Metuchen, NJ: Scarecrow Press, 1981), which contains 831 book titles, but no journal articles. The introduction lays out a history of technical style manuals. The other 2 bibliographies cover both books and journal articles: Society of Technical Writers and Publishers, *An Annotated Bibliography on Technical Writing, Editing, Graphics, and Publishing: 1950-1965,* Theresa A. Philler, Ruth K. Hersh, and Helen V. Carlson, eds. (Washington, DC: Society of Technical Writers and Publishers, and the Carnegie Library of Pittsburgh, [1966]); and Sarojini Balachandran, *Technical Writings: A Bibliography* (Urbana, IL: American Business Communication Association, c1977), which is unnumbered but annotated, covers the years 1966–77, is indexed and includes microforms. The latest books on technical writing are found under the subject "Technical writing" in the current edition of *Subject Guide to Books in Print* (New York: Bowker) and by consulting the reviews of new books in the *Journal of Technical Writing and Communication* (Farmingdale, NY: Baywood Publishing).

ARRANGEMENT

This guide is arranged alphabetically by subject preceded by a section of manuals for general use. These selected commercial, government, and university press style manuals are the most used of all the manuals. Outside of the manuals found in the general section are those specifically for individual disciplines, such as biology, education, geology, law, mathematics, physics, and psychology. Writers in one of the specialized fields should consult the subject style manuals as well as one or more of the general manuals.

Under each subject, manuals are arranged alphabetically by compiler. Three kinds of information are provided for each entry: bibliographic citation, a description of the contents, and observations on the bibliographic style. In some cases, an evaluation of the manual has been made. The bibliographic citation consists of author, title, edition (if any), place of publication, publisher, date of publication, pagination, International Standard Book Number, Library of Congress card number, and price (if any). Prices for most commercial titles come from *Books in Print,* 1982–83 edition; *British Books in Print,* 1982 edition; and *Canadian Books in Print,* 1981 edition. If the manual has a bibliographic history, this information is included in notes under the bibliographic citation paragraph. There follow a description of the contents and the paragraph on "Bibliographic style" enumerating the elements of a bibliography as recommended by that particular manual. In selective cases, additional evaluative comments have been added to conclude the entry. An index of names (corporate and personal), subjects, and titles is provided.

HISTORY NOTE

The contemporary style manual is a product of 300 years of development that was dominated by printers until the end of the nineteenth century. German printers issued guides to printing in 1608, 1653, and 1673.[4] The first printer's manual in English was Joseph Moxon's *Mechanik Exercises* (London: 1683), "a teach yourself series" described as "the first comprehensive manual in any language."[5] In the last half of the eighteenth

---

[4]Philip Gaskell, Giles Barber, and Georgina Warrilow, "An Annotated List of Printers Manuals to 1850," *Journal of the Printing Historical Society* 4 (1968): 24–25.

[5]Gaskell, et al., p. 13.

century, 3 additional style manuals in English were published. However, the first 40 years of the nineteenth century witnessed the publication of 20 printer's manuals: 13 in the United Kingdom and 7 in the United States.[6] No one has discussed this period of printer's manuals better than Charles H. Timperley, who traces the history of manuals from 1755 to 1838, the publication date of his *The Printers' Manual* (London).[7] Timperley's manual is a printer's manual and not a style guide; most of the slim volume is devoted to composing, imposing, correcting in metal, and scales of prices for a compositor's work. He also provides short sections on punctuation, spelling, capitals and small capitals, accented letters, numeral letters, italics, signs, and symbols. The manual also contains elements on italics and foreign alphabets (Hebrew and Greek). Timperley's contribution to the history of the style manual lies in his short introductory essay on the origins and similarities of 6 of the style manuals published from 1800 to 1838. He makes it quite clear that 4 of the 6 borrow or plagiarize extensive passages from earlier manuals. He concludes his remarks: "Thus it plainly appears, that each writer of a *Printers' Grammar* has not hesitated to take from his predecessor all that he thought requisite to form his own."[8] It is clear from Timperley's account that the nineteenth century printer's manuals were the product of many hands. None of them, in either the United Kingdom or the United States, survived the turn of the century.

In 1864, Horace Hart, member of the London Association of Correctors of the Press, and later printer to Oxford University, began the compilation of his "Rules," which were finally published by the university in 1893.[9] In later editions, Sir J. A. H. Murray and Dr. Henry Bradley, editors of the *Oxford English Dictionary*, revised and approved all spellings. *Hart's Rules* is prescriptive and is primarily for printers although its continued success—its 38th edition appeared in 1978—suggests a widespread utility in the United Kingdom.[10]

In January 1892, William A. Croffut, head of the Editorial Division of the United States Geological Survey, authored *Suggestions for the Preparation of Manuscript and Illustrations for Publication by the U.S. Geolog-*

---

[6]Gaskell, et al., pp. 14–19.

[7]Charles H. Timperley, *The Printers' Manual* (London: H. Johnson, 1838; reprint ed., London: Gregg Press, 1965), p. 3.

[8]Timperley, p. 3.

[9]Oxford University Press, *Hart's Rules for Compositors and Readers at the University Press, Oxford*, 38th ed. (Oxford: Oxford University Press, [c1978]).

[10]For additional information, *see* item 106.

ical Survey, a short pamphlet of 15 pages.[11] Unlike *Hart's Rules,* Croffut includes practical information that might be of value to anyone preparing for publication. Croffut's *Suggestions* are noteworthy because they are the first published statement of style for a department of the federal government of the United States.

In 1894, the United States Government Printing Office issued its first *Manual of Style.* It is not unlike *Hart's Rules* in its layout of lists: double words, termination of words, Indian names, county names, and an especially long list of geographic names approved by the United States Board on Geographic Names. The 1903 edition limits its "Suggestions to authors" to one page following the table of contents.[12] The present USGPO *Style Manual* retains its format for lists.[13] Although authors and editors do use it as a reference book, the USGPO *Style Manual* has not become a national style manual the way the Australian government manual has.

The process by which the printer's manual evolved into the editor's and author's manual is best shown by comparing the various editions of *The Chicago Manual of Style* published by the University of Chicago Press. The Chicago manual was first published in 1906, and although there are sections of the manual for editors and authors, the printer's specimens of type dominate the last third of the manual for the next 63 years. Gradually, the section on specimens of type diminishes from well over 160 pages in the eleventh edition (1949) to 20 pages in the twelfth edition (1969), until it disappears entirely in the thirteenth edition (1982). During the manual's first 76 years, the sections under "style" increase gradually, providing more information on punctuation, bibliographies, indexes, spelling, and footnotes, all grouped together by the manual's editors under the term "style." With the appearance of the thirteenth edition in 1982, the thrust of the manual has moved toward the problems of the author and the editor, and away from those of the printer. The section on type specimens has been replaced with a new chapter entitled "Composition, Printing and Binding," which discusses the printing process in the twentieth century in 2 aspects: the hand processes and the machine processes.[14] This change in

---

11William A. Croffut, *Suggestions for the Preparation of Manuscript and Illustrations for Publication by the U.S. Geological Survey* (Washington, DC: USGPO, 1892).

12United States, Government Printing Office, *Manual of Style for Use in Composition and Proof Reading* (Washington, DC: USGPO, 1903), p. 5.

13United States, Government Printing Office, *Style Manual,* revised ed. (Washington, DC USGPO, 1973).

14University of Chicago Press, *The Chicago Manual of Style,* 13th ed. (Chicago: 1982), pp. 585–644.

emphasis is the opposite of the practice found in style manuals of the nineteenth century where the concerns of the printer and the emphasis on specimen type dominate format and content. The present layout of *The Chicago Manual of Style* attempts to balance the needs of the editor and author for more detailed information on points of style with the traditional needs of the printer for technical data on the publishing process. Today, the Chicago style is used by at least 95 commercial and academic presses in North America, including most university presses.

The spread of Chicago style has not been entirely dependent on the appearance and revisions of *The Chicago Manual of Style*. Beginning in 1937, the University of Chicago Press published *A Manual for Writers of Dissertations* by Kate L. Turabian. The fourth edition of this guide, now called *A Manual for Writers of Term Papers, Theses, and Dissertations*, is widely used by academic institutions in the United States.[15] The manual's long-term success has led to its 1982 publication in the United Kingdom under the title *A Manual for Writers of Research Papers, Theses, and Dissertations*, in an edition prepared by John E. Spink.[16] The legal section has been changed substantially to accommodate British usage; otherwise, Turabian's manual may rapidly become an important vehicle for the establishment of an international style for English-speaking countries at the academic level.

The variety of style manuals in the English-speaking world currently emphasizes local house style. However, according to one British observer, the enforcement of a house style is impractical because of the publication of coeditions and the reprint of editions prepared by offset lithography outside the publishing house.[17] This observation indicates a change in attitude that may be important for the future of publishing style, which may be determined by the marketplace rather than by the author, the editor, or the publisher.

STANDARDIZATION OF BIBLIOGRAPHY

Since World War II, the International Organization for Standardization (ISO) and the offices of national standards organizations such as the

---

[15]Kate L. Turabian, *A Manual for Writers of Term Papers, Theses, and Dissertations*, 4th ed. (Chicago: University of Chicago Press, [1973]).

[16]Kate L. Turabian, *A Manual for Writers of Research Papers, Theses, and Dissertations*. British ed. prepared by John E. Spink (London: Heinemann, 1982).

[17]W. Roger Smith, Peter Davies, letter to the compiler, July 16, 1981.

British Standards Institution (BSI) and the American National Standards Institute, Inc. (ANSI) have issued standards on publishing and the transfer of information. In particular, ANSI has concentrated on romanization, book format, and bibliographic interchange. One of the latest to appear is the *American National Standard for Bibliographic References,*[18] which is currently the focus of much activity moving toward the standardization of bibliographic entries at the international level. The international community has for some time advanced the idea of international cooperation through the publication of ISO standards, which have been adopted whole or in part by individual countries. It is in the field of medicine that bibliographic anarchy has given way to the bibliographic system outlined in the *American National Standard for Bibliographic References.* At their 1977 meeting in Vancouver, the editors of 19 medical journals from Canada, the United Kingdom, and the United States agreed to adopt the *Uniform Requirements for Manuscripts Submitted to Biomedical Journals,* amended in 1978 and known informally as the "Vancouver declaration, revised," which is a slightly revised version of the *American National Standard for Bibliographic References.*[19] Perhaps the most important fact is not that the 19 journal editors adopted a standard, but that *Index Medicus* adopted the *American National Standard for Bibliographic References* effective January 1, 1980. Fifty-five organizations in the United States had approved the standard before it was adopted in Vancouver. A few of them are major organizations publishing their own style manuals, namely the American Chemical Society, the American Institute of Physics, and the Council of Biology Editors, among others.[20] With the broadening of support to include major organizations outside the medical field, it is expected that other institutions in the United States and abroad will join with those adhering to the *American National Standard for Bibliographic References,* or its appearance in the international version, the *Uniform Requirements for Manuscripts Submitted to Biomedical Journals.*

---

[18]American National Standards Institute, *American National Standard for Bibliographic References* (ANSI Z39.29–1977) (New York: 1977); object of a review article by D. W. Krummel and John Bruce Howell, "Bibliographic Standards and Style," *Scholarly Publishing* 10 (April 1979): 223–40.

[19]International Steering Committee of Medical Editors, "Uniform Requirements for Manuscripts Submitted to Biomedical Journals," *British Medical Journal* 1 (1979): 532–35.

[20]"Change of *Index Medicus* Citation Format," *Index Medicus* 22 (May 1981): viii.

General Manuals

COMMERCIAL PUBLISHERS

1. Allen (George) & Unwin Ltd. *Author's guide to typescript preparation, house style, and proof correction.* London: [1973]. 32p. ISBN 0-04-655010-0.

> Divided into 3 major parts: typescript preparation, house style, and proof correction.

> Bibliographic style: author separated from italicized title of book by comma. Imprint, including only publisher, edition, and date of publication, is placed within parentheses followed by a period. Periodical articles are placed within single quotes, separated from the italicized title of the periodical by a comma. There follow another comma, volume designation, date within parentheses, and pages (p.).

> An attractive, well-printed manual.

2. Allyn and Bacon, Inc. *Author's guide.* Boston: [c1973]. 60p. illus.

> Divided into 13 chapters: 1. planning, 2. from title page to index, 3. manuscript preparation, 4. questions of style, 5. permissions, 6. libel and other dangers, 7. illustrations, 8. preparing a book of readings, 9. reviewing, editing, estimating, 10. proofreading and the final stages, 11. indexing, 12. reprints and new editions, and 13. some problems of multiple authorship. Indexed.

> Bibliographic style: "Our official house style is that of the University of Chicago Press, *A Manual of Style*, 12th edition (Chicago: 1969). . . . Our psychology books deviate from Chicago style and follow the *Publication Manual* published by the American Psychological Association. In physics we follow the *Style Manual* of the American Institute of Physics."

3. Arnold-Heinemann Publishers (India). *Notes for authors.* [New Delhi: 1976.] 16p.

Divided into 8 parts: preparing the manuscript, house style, illustrations, permissions, proofs, making an index, bound copies—and after, and standard proof marks. Under "House style": "Our authorities are *Chambers Everyday Dictionary* and *Collins Authors and Printers Dictionary.*"

Bibliographic style: Harvard style with date in parentheses coming after author's name followed by the title of the book in italics, then place and publisher. Uses abbreviated titles for periodicals.

4. Beetham, Beverley. *Macmillan Company of Canada: Editorial style manual.* [Toronto: Macmillan Company of Canada], 1977. 26 leaves. Bibliography: leaf 25.

Divided into 23 sections: handling of various book parts, proofs, punctuation, spelling, hyphenation, capitalization, numbers, names, foreign languages, italics, small caps, illustrations, captions, tables, abbreviations, extracts, notes and footnotes, bibliographies, indexes, company reference routes, design mark-up, aberrations, and bibliography.

Bibliographic style: order of elements is given. For examples, the author is referred to *The Chicago Manual of Style* and to Marjorie E. Skillin and Robert M. Gay's *Words into Type.*

An interesting, original piece of work that would prove useful to other Canadian publishers. Includes a list of Canadian names and newspapers.

5. Benjamin/Cummings Publishing Co. *Author's guide.* [Menlo Park, CA: c1981.] 93p. (loose-leaf) with 3 holes for ring binder. ISBN 0-8053-9931-3; LC card 80-25395. Bibliography: p. 90.

Divided into 2 parts. Part 1, preparing your manuscript, includes 6 chapters: 1. organization, 2. planning and writing, 3. legal matters, 4. reviews and revising, 5. preparing the manuscript, and 6. the art manuscript. Part 2, making your book, contains 4 chapters: 7. words become type, 8. proofs, 9. the index, and 10. the finished book. Included are 3 appendixes: A. reprints and new editions, B. supplements, and C. anthologies and readers. A glossary of "terms as they are used in textbook publishing" is provided. The bibliography includes books about writing and preparing a manuscript, style manuals, books about publishing, general reference books, and technical reference books. The guide concludes with a detailed index.

Bibliographic style: no bibliographic style is presented.

Benjamin/Cummings, a subsidiary of Addison-Wesley, publishes textbooks in the fields of astronomy, biology, chemistry, mathematics, physics, and anthropology. The chapter on the art manuscript is a detailed treatment of a subject not so extensively covered in other style manuals. Also of interest is an abridged list of "McGraw-Hill's guidelines for equal treatment of the sexes." The manual is well designed, easy to use, and up to date.

6. Cape (Jonathan) Limited. *House style*. [London: 197–?.] 28p.

Divided into 9 sections: spelling, punctuation, italics, capitals, abbreviations, numerals, dates, layout, and other potential pitfalls. There follow a section on proofreading with marks used in proofreading and an index.

Bibliographic style: no bibliographic style is presented. Footnote style is author's initials; last name; title in italics; publisher, place, and date of publication in parentheses; and roman numerals designating volume and chapter. Periodical articles have author's initials, last name, title in single quotes, title of periodical in italics, volume numbers in roman, dates in parentheses, and finally, inclusive pages.

Attractively printed with a very clear section on marks used in proofreading.

7. Currie, Elizabeth A. *A guide for authors and editors*. Prepared for Academic Press by Elizabeth Adams Currie in cooperation with the Book Production Department. New York: Academic Press, 1966. [iv], 57, [2]p.

Divided into 2 major parts, which are further subdivided. Part I is preparation of manuscript and includes sections on deadlines, typing, completeness, outline of chapter contents, headings and subheadings, corrections and insertions in the manuscript, tables, illustrations, legends, footnotes, references, and permission to reproduce copyrighted material. Part II is how to deal with proofs, a 7-page detailed examination of the problem. Included are 9 appendixes: A. spelling and terminology, B. abbreviations, C. mathematical material, D. chemical formulas, E. nomenclature of organisms, F. suggestions for editors of treatises and similar volumes, G. suggestions for editors of advances and other serial volumes, H. suggestions for editors of symposium volumes, and I. summary of the steps in converting manuscripts into printed books. No index.

Bibliographic style: 4 systems are presented dependent on footnote style: 1. "Name and Date," i.e., Harvard style, 2. numbering system with list of references alphabetized, 3. numbering system following sequence of mention in text, and 4. ''Letter and Number System'': ''In the reference list, entries are arranged alphabetically by authors' surnames and each one is preceded by a capital letter corresponding to the first letter of the surname of the first author, followed by an arabic number corresponding to the position of the reference in the list for that letter.'' For example:

> A1. Abrams, I. M., and Dickinson, B. N., *Ind. Eng. Chem. 41*, 2521 (1949).
> B1. Bessis, M., and Breton-Gorius, J., *Compt. Rend. 251*, 465 (1960).

An interesting detailed manual that needs to be revised and reformatted. Its present layout of indented letters and numbers and its lack of index make it difficult to use.

8. Davis (F. A.) Co. *The preparation of a manuscript: Information for authors.* [Philadelphia, PA: 1976.] 20p.

''The topics covered in this booklet are: submitting a manuscript, handling galley proofs, page proofs, and new editions. A glossary is also included.''

Bibliographic style: unique. Colon separates author's inverted names from italicized title. Edition (ed.) precedes number. Then follow the publisher, place of publication, and date of publication, all separated from one another with commas. Periodical articles have last name first, followed by initials of first and middle names. Journal titles are abbreviated according to those in *Index Medicus*. The abbreviated title is followed by the volume number, colon, page number, and date.

F. A. Davis also issues *Guidelines for Preparing a Book Proposal* (4 leaves).

9. Dent (J. M.) & Sons (Canada). *The preparation of manuscripts: Notes for the guidance of authors.* Don Mills, Ontario: [197–?]. 19p.

Divided into 14 parts: initial planning; the physical appearance of the manuscript; duplicate copies of the manuscript; illustrations; credit lines and captions; format and cover designs; quotation of copyright material; bibliographies; headings; accuracy, consistency, and style; the production stage; summary; a final word; and proofreader's marks.

Bibliographic style: gives an example for a book that is identical to that presented in *The Chicago Manual of Style*.

10. Dodd, Mead & Co. *Dodd, Mead author's manual: Some suggestions for authors about the preparation of manuscripts and the reading of proof.* New York: [197–?]. 16p.

Divided into 4 parts: the manuscript, consists of the paper; typing; numbering and fastening the pages; additions and corrections; front matter; quotations; printed copy in manuscript; footnotes; bibliography; illustrations, charts, maps, tables; captions; credit lines; and revised editions. Part 2, editorial style, consists of spelling, punctuation, abbreviations, numbers, and italics. Proofreading includes galley proofs and page proofs. A section on the index concludes the manual.

Bibliographic style: follows *The Chicago Manual of Style* in all aspects of editorial style.

11. Elwood, DeElda. *The Doubleday manual of style.* Garden City, NY: Doubleday, 1972. 80p.

Includes 12 unnumbered chapters: a word about this manual, do's and don'ts of copy editing, spelling, abbreviations, numbers, possessives and apostrophes, capitalization, italics, punctuation, footnotes, bibliographies, and some general rules. There is one page of proofreader's marks and one on how to correct proof. A detailed index completes the volume.

Bibliographic style: "References listed in the bibliography of a book should include the author's name, title of work, place of publication, publisher and year. Sometimes the number of pages is also included, as well as other descriptive matter." Follows *The Chicago Manual of Style* except for pagination of periodical articles, which is wanting.

Particularly strong on points of punctuation.

12. Grant, Fern B. *Guidelines for writers of letters, themes, memorandums, pamphlets, news stories, minutes of meetings, reports, and books.* [Quezon City: New Day Publishers of the Christian Literature Society of the Philippines, c1975.] viii, 101p. LC card 78-315848.

Divided into 7 parts: 1. making the writing process less difficult, 2. using English correctly and with style, 3. writing for varied purposes, 4. submitting material for publication, 5. making the contract for the publication of a book, 6. producing, publicizing, and selling the book: the author's role, and 7. publishing by amateurs.

Bibliographic style: generally follows *The Chicago Manual of Style* except for not italicizing subtitles of books and for slight changes in pagination, e.g., pp. 36–45 in place of Chicago's: 36–45.

"The reader will notice that no reference is made to special problems encountered in writing master's theses and doctoral dissertations. Each educational institution prepares its own specifications for these; besides, excellent guides for producing these are available in Manila book stores." The chapter on publishing by amateurs in the Philippines and the lengthy discussion of bibliographic style are important contributions to the growth of publishing in developing countries.

13. Gulf Publishing Co. Book Division. *Author's handbook.* Houston, TX: [c1976]. vi, 38p. ISBN 0-87201-048-1. $2.95.

Divided into 6 sections: what should your manuscript contain?, copy preparation, editing, design and production, group authorships and seminar proceedings, revisions, and promotion and marketing. A useful glossary of publishing terms appears at the end (pp. 31–38).

Bibliographic style: identical to that presented in *The Chicago Manual of Style*, except for the months of the year, which are abbreviated in the *Authors' Handbook*.

14. *Handbook for Indian writers, 1975.* Edited by H. K. Kaul. [New Delhi]: Munshiram Manoharal Publishers, [1975, c1974]. xii, 324p. LC card 75-905108; Rs60. Bibliography: pp. 190–294.

Divided into 2 parts: part 1, called "Papers," includes a set of 28 essays on publishing in India: On being a writer, by Ka Naa Subramanyam; Copyright: a perspective, by S. C. Chukla; Law of libel, by A. B. N. Sinha; Censorship, by Justice G. D. Khosla; The writer and the publisher: general introduction, by R. E. Hawkins; The publisher's contract, by J. M. Mukhi; Editor, author and publisher, by Samuel Israel; Paperbacks in India: what an author should know about them, by D. N. Malhotra; State aids to the writer, by Abul Hasan; What are you doing about selling my book? an answer, by N. A. O'Brien; The syndicated column, by A. R. Vyas; The marketing of articles about India in American magazines, by John E. Frazer; Reporting for Indian newspapers, by Dilip Mukherjee; The editor, by Ravi Dayal; Copyediting and house style, by Narendra Kumar; Document bibliography, by H. K. Kaul; On indexing, by T. N. Rajan; The art of book reviewing, by V. V. John; Translation of Indian literature into English, by Dr. Prabhakar Machwe; Radio and the writer, by P. C. Chatterji; The writer and television, by N. L. Chowla; Getting your book printed, by A. Azim; The art of binding of books, by Y. P. Kathpalia; Illustrations and reproduction methods, by Kuldeep Singh Jus; Designing a book, by Dilip Chowdhury; Cultural papers and boards, by Dr. Roshan L. Bhargava; Economics of book publishing: cost analysis, by N. R. Subramanian; and Preparation and submission of manuscripts, by H. K. Kaul. Part 2 is a reference directory of Indian publishers, journals, and magazines. It includes sections entitled Who's who: a selected list of Indian writers; societies and institutions of interest to authors, journalists and artists; literary, news and press agencies; literary prizes and awards; and other services, as well as a select bibliography and a journalists' calendar. Appendixes contain proofreading symbols, a form for the registration of copyright, a form for the deposit of books, a confidential market survey and a memorandum of agreement, a form for the registration of a magazine, and a list of the workshop papers included in the handbook. Indexed.

Bibliographic style: as presented by H. K. Kaul in his essay "Document Bibliography," the style for books is identical to that presented in *The Chicago Manual of Style*. For a periodical article, the style is author's name, title of the article, name of the periodical (unabbreviated and in italics), volume and number of the periodical, date of the particular number, and page numbers of the particular citation. Latin abbreviations such as ibid, op. cit., and loc. cit. are acceptable.

Especially important for its essays on editing and house style in India, and for its bibliography.

15. Harper & Row. College Dept. *Harper & Row author's manual*. New York: [c1976]. vii, 40p. ISBN 06-360110-9. LC card 76-356014. (Out of print; new ed. in preparation.)

Divided into 2 parts: preparing the manuscript, which includes sections on the master manuscript, text elements, technical manuscripts, permissions, illustrations, revisions, anthologies and reprinted material, front matter, and the index; and producing the book, which includes sections on copyediting, design and sample pages, cut dummy, galleys, pages, front matter and index pages, author's alterations, and how to mark proof.

Bibliographic style: no bibliographic style is presented.

16. Heinemann (William), Ltd. *Notes for authors*. [3rd ed.]. London: Heinemann, [1980]. iv, 29p. (First ed. 1966; 2nd ed. 1969.)

Includes 25 topics treated in a concise manner: prospective authors, presentation of typescript, presentation of text, illustrations, tables, graphs, reproducing examination questions, house style, technical editing, punctuation, capitals, hyphens, singulars and plurals, numbers, dates, currency, legal works, notation and abbreviation of units, the SI system of units, mathematics, chemical texts, proofs, making an index, bound copies—and after, and a conclusion. Indexed.

Bibliographic style: "These [bibliographical references] are useless unless complete and should contain: author's name and initials [full capitals]; the full title of the article or book [in italics]; if a book, town of origin, the name of the publisher, year of publication [all in parentheses]; or if an article, the name of the journal [capitalized and abbreviated] or other source, year of publication, volume number, page numbers."

"Our authorities are *The Oxford Dictionary* and Collins's *Author's and Printers' Dictionary* (also published by the Oxford University Press). The latter is strongly recommended to our authors: it contains many useful spellings and abbreviations and is the standard guide to typographical practice. Hart's *Rules for Compositors and Readers at the University Press, Oxford* supplies the answers to many irritating queries, likewise."

Succinct presentation of the elements of style for the author. Frequently, reference is made to a useful British standard or appropriate reference book.

17. International Universities Press. *Style sheet.* New York: [197–?]. 7 leaves. Photocopy.

Divided into 2 parts: preparation of manuscripts including special typing instructions, footnotes, headings and subheadings, tables and charts, and documentation including references.

Bibliographic style: Harvard, with 12 sample references.

18. Jacaranda Wiley, Ltd. *Style manual for authors and editors.* [Brisbane]: Jacaranda Press, 1975. 68 leaves. Photocopy.

A pragmatic manual important for its prescriptive advice on Australian usage. Includes sections on "What to do with your manuscript, Arranging letters, English into American, Spelling demons, Alternative spellings, Unenglish plurals, Apostrophe, Indefinite article, [and] Foreign words and phrases." Also provided are discussions of "Capital initials, Hypens, Division of words, Abbreviations and reference words, Punctuation, Quotations (punctuation), Numerals, The book's progress (guidelines for editors), Correcting proofs, Managing words, Quotations (documentation), [and] Editorial exercises."

"Jacaranda Press house style follows that of the University of Chicago Press, *A Manual of Style,* twelfth edition (1969)." However, in spelling, British usage is preferred.

Bibliographic style: "In general reference lists, Jacaranda Press follows the Chicago simplified style for the humanities and in science texts the Chicago science style."

A detailed manual with clear explanations. Presently under revision.

19. Little, Brown and Co. College Division. *Author's guide.* Boston: [c1979]. xi, 84p. LC card 78-70882. $3.95.

Divided into 9 chapters: 1. manuscript preparation, 2. the elements of a manuscript, 3. permissions, 4. front matter, 5. preparing an index, 6. revisions, 7. anthologies, 8. producing the book, and 9. teacher's manual. Indexed.

Bibliographic style: allowing for minor changes in punctuation, the bibliographic style follows closely *The Chicago Manual of Style.*

Interesting for its chapter on teacher's manuals, a topic that is not well covered elsewhere. Sample pages are used throughout this guide, which is laid out well with ample spacing between paragraphs and in the margins.

20. *Longman Cheshire's guide for authors, editors, designers, typesetters and printers.* [Melbourne]: Longman Cheshire, [ca. 1977]. 50p.

Divided into 4 parts: preparation of manuscript, preparation of artwork, Australian studies, and publication details. Part 1 includes sections on presentation of the manuscript, illustrations, tables, headings, quotations, bibliographies and references (endnotes), mathematics and numbers, indexes, consistency, general typing instructions, further points of style, and useful references. The remainder of the book provides examples of preliminary pages, part pages, text, notes, a bibliography, and an index from an *Australian Studies* title.

Bibliographic style: author, followed by titles of books in italics, name of publisher, place of publication, and date of publication. Periodical articles have author, followed by title of the article in single quotes, title of the periodical in italics, volume and issue number, date, and pagination, all separated from each other by commas. The Harvard reference system is presented as an alternative means of citation.

Useful for its samples of the parts of a book. Brief presentation of style. The New Zealand office issues *Manuscript Preparation,* an 11-page (unnumbered) document, to supplement the guide.

21. McGraw-Hill Book Co. *The McGraw-Hill author's book.* New York: [c1968]. 74p. ISBN 07-045051-X; LC card 68-6295. $3.00. (First published in 1922 with title: *A few suggestions to McGraw-Hill authors;* unnumbered editions published in 1926, 1929, 1935, 1944, 1948, 1952, and 1955.)

Divided into 9 unnumbered chapters: the publishing partnership, gathering materials and writing the manuscript, permissions and copyrights, preparing the manuscript for the publisher, the production process, how to prepare the index, preparing a revision, how we market your book, and this is McGraw-Hill. Indexed.

Bibliographic style: unique: "Some textbooks contain extensive bibliographies. The style of the bibliography should match that of footnotes, with 2 exceptions: (1) names of authors are inverted (for ease of alphabetizing); when there are coauthors, the name of only the senior author is inverted, and (2) a colon rather than a comma separates the author's name from the title. Here is an example of a bibliographic entry:

Adrian, Charles R., and Charles Press: *The American Political Process,* McGraw-Hill Book Company, New York, 1965, pp. 109–114.

"Style, in publishing, refers to the consistent use of an accepted standard for punctuation, capitalization, abbreviation, footnote and bibliographic form, the writing of numbers, and so on. We urge you to adopt uniform and well-established forms in preparing your manuscript. . . .

"Rules of style acceptable in one discipline may not apply in another. Most publishers combine the best-established usages to form their own 'house style.' McGraw-Hill style standards are respected throughout the publishing world. They are high standards that have evolved over the years through constant contact with authors, style authorities, scientific and technical organizations, professional associations, and so on. Our editors keep up to date with changes in style and adjust McGraw-Hill's standards whenever the changes appear to be well founded and likely to endure."

The section on copyright is out of date and needs revision. Two booklets: *Guidelines for Equal Treatment of the Sexes in McGraw-Hill Book Company Publications* and *Guidelines for Fair Representation of Disabled People in McGraw-Hill Book Company Publications* need to be incorporated in the author's book.

21a. *The McGraw-Hill style manual: A concise guide for writers and editors.* Edited by Marie Longyear. New York: McGraw-Hill [c1983]. xiii,

333 p. ISBN 0-07-038676-5; LC card 82-195; $19.95. Bibliography: pp. 301–07.

Divided into 4 parts of 13 chapters: part 1, general standards, consisting of the following chapters: 1. spelling, hyphenation, italics and quotation marks, 2. capitalization, 3. numbers, measurements, and abbreviations, 4. extracts, lists, and other elements of the text, 5. reference material, and 6. tables. Part 2, technical standards, consists of the following chapters: 7. mathematics, electronics, and computer sciences, and 8. chemistry and life sciences. Part 3 consists of the following chapters: 9. grammar and usage, and 10. punctuation. Part 4, from manuscript to book, consists of the following chapters: 11. preparing the manuscript, 12. copy editing and proofreading, and 13. making the index. There is a detailed index.

Bibliographic style: "The style of the bibliography should match that of the footnotes, with two exceptions: 1. Names of authors are inverted in an alphabetized list; when a work has more than one author, only the name of the first author is inverted; 2. a colon rather than a comma usually separates the author's name (or authors' names) from the title." McGraw-Hill bibliographic style is unique in placing the name of the publisher before the place of publication. Only 5 examples of bibliographic style are presented.

This manual attempts to be a comprehensive guide to all aspects and problems of style. It is particularly good for its approach to mathematical, electronic, and computer science notation and the presentation of chemical symbols. Much of its prescriptive comment details solutions to problems faced by both editors and writers. Marie Longyear notes in her preface: "The recommendations set forth here are especially suited for general nonfiction; for educational texts at the high school, vocational school, business school, college, and postgraduate levels; and for professional texts and reference books in almost every field."

This detailed style manual is a thorough exposition of the style used by one of the major publishers in the United States. It could easily complement the major style manuals, and it is especially good for editors.

22. Macmillan Press. *Advice to authors: Academic and reference books in the arts and social sciences.* [London: 1979.] 23p. ISBN 0-333-21791-8.

Divided into 13 parts: procedure, the typescript, the structure of a book, copyright material, compilations, house style, special sorts, tables, illustrations, endnotes, references, proofs, and indexes.

Bibliographic style: dependent upon "references." Periodical articles use single quote for title and roman numerals are used for volume numbers. Imprint enclosed in parentheses.

Clearly enumerates and explains its own house style.

23. *Manual for writers: A handbook for authors and editors, with special reference to the requirements of writers in Pakistan.* Compiled by Rafiq Khawar; edited by Akhtar Husain Raipuri. Karachi: National Book Centre of Pakistan, [1974]. 121p. LC card 75-938527. Rs 15.00.

"The present Manual prepared with assistance and encouragement from Unesco is a pioneering work in Urdu [*sic*] compiled by a prolific writer with ample experience in almost every branch of writing: creative, scholarly, educational or motivating."

Divided into 10 chapters: how to write; writing for children; educational books; general readers, literature, journalism, mass media, theatre, radio, TV, screen; translation; the manuscript–preparation; the publisher; editing; production; incentives, and opportunities.

Bibliographic style: chapter 6 on manuscript preparation includes information on the text, with details on bibliographies and references. Sequence of elements in the citation is author's surname and initials, title, edition, place of publication, publisher's name, year of publication, volume, and pagination.

24. Merrill (Charles E.) Publishing Co. College Division. *The publishing process: A book for our author.* Columbus, OH: [c1975]. iv, 124p. illus. ISBN 0-675-08675-2. (Earlier editions 1958, c1955; 1964.)

Divided into 7 chapters: 1. beginning your book, 2. preparing your manuscript, 3. preparing your technical manuscript, 4. illustrating your manuscript, 5. copyright and permissions, 6. producing your book, and 7. preparing manuals, reprints, and revisions. Indexed.

Bibliographic style: follows *The Chicago Manual of Style.* Use of other subject style manuals, e.g., the *Publication Manual of the American Psychological Association* and the *MLA Handbook for Writers of Research Papers, Theses, and Dissertations,* is permitted.

Good chapters on illustrations, symbols, the international system of units, mathematical equations, and chemical symbols. Easy-to-read, step-by-step approach to the publishing of a book. A well-designed and well-bound manual. The chapter on copyright and permissions is out of date, and some of the information is incorrect.

25. Nicholson, Margaret. *A practical style guide for authors and editors.* New York: Holt, Rinehart and Winston, [1971, c1967]. xiii, 143p. ISBN 0-03-085491-1; LC card 67-10739. $1.75. Bibliography: pp. 130–34.

Divided into 16 unnumbered parts: the author's responsibility; the editor's responsibility; front matter; back matter; quotations; sources, citations, footnotes; bibliographies; index; proofreading; copyright, fair use, permissions; abbreviations; capitalization; italics; numbers and figures; punctuation pitfalls; and the reference shelf. Indexed.

Bibliographic style: cites a variety of styles with samples and critically annotates each example. No one style is recommended.

A loosely organized manual primarily directed toward editors. In place of a discussion of the various points of style, examples are presented and subsequently explained. Not easy to use as a reference work because running heads are placed at the inner margin and unnumbered chapters are not subdivided by topic.

26. *Notes for authors on the preparation of typescripts [for] Ernest Benn, incorporating Charles Knight Publications.* London: Ernest Benn, [197–?]. 7p.

Refers authors to *Hart's Rules.* Otherwise includes information on dates, titles, quotation marks, quotations, foreign words, numbers, British usage, hyphens, capitalization, punctuation, footnotes, quotes, permissions, and illustrations.

Bibliographic style: for books, author followed by colon, title in italics, place of publication, and date. Publisher not given. No periodical articles are cited.

Ernest Benn also issues *Proof Correction: Some Notes for the Guidance of Authors and Editors* (4 unnumbered pages).

27. Olsen, Udia G. *Preparing the manuscript.* [9th ed.] Boston: The Writer, Inc., [c1978]. iv, 154p. ISBN 0-87116-115-X; LC card 78-13577. $6.95. (First ed. 1939; 2nd ed. 1946; 3rd ed. 1951; 4th ed. 1961; 5th ed. 1965; 6th ed. 1968; 7th ed. 1972; 8th ed. 1976.) Bibliography: p. 150.

Divided into 14 parts: tools and materials, typing the manuscript, checking and correcting, grammar and composition, spelling, capitalization, punctuation, submitting for publication, proofreading, making an index, copyright, author's rights, permissions, and marketing your manuscript. Indexed.

Bibliographic style: presents examples that follow *The Chicago Manual of Style.*

Although primarily for the commercial or professional writer, this manual is well written and very readable and is recommended for step-by-step instruction in the mechanical preparation of material for publication.

28. Open Court Publishing Co. *A guide to the preparation of manuscripts*. [La Salle, IL]: 1977. 9 leaves. (At head of title: ME-Editorial Style 3. Photocopy.)

". . . based on the Chicago *Manual of Style*."

Divided into 6 parts: paper; typing the manuscript including general guidelines, product identification and page numbers, headings, extracts, special matter, word division; corrections and alterations; retyping a copyedited manuscript; common copyediting marks; and sample corrected tear sheet.

Bibliographic style: though no bibliographic style is presented, presumably follows *The Chicago Manual of Style*.

29. Pergamon Press. *Style notes for authors for the preparation of camera-ready manuscripts*. Oxford: [1979]. 13p.

Includes 10 unnumbered sections: instructions to the typist; tables, formulae, mathematical symbols, etc.; figure captions and table headings; illustrations/figures; headings, chapter titles and page numbers; footnotes; references; indexes; order of preliminary and end pages; and text. There follow 4 specimen pages. The booklet concludes with a list of preferred abbreviations of journal titles and a list of Pergamon preferred abbreviations.

Bibliographic style: follows Harvard style. Concise statement of house style with examples.

Pergamon also issues a similar publication entitled *Style Notes for Authors for the Preparation of Camera-ready Manuscripts: Symposium Publications* (1979, 17p.).

30. *Pitman guide to authors*. [London]: Pitman Publishing, [ca. 1975]. 40p. Bibliography: p. 40.

Divided into 9 parts: introduction, presentation of typescript, preparation of copy for new editions and revised impressions, style, illustrations, tables, references, index, and proof correction. Includes 3 appendixes: 1. copyright material, 2. scientific and other complex scripts (symbols, units, mathematics, chemistry, prefixes, analyses, structural formulae, taxonomy, biology, geology, astronomy, book-keeping and accountancy, and law), and 3. bibliography. No index.

Bibliographic style: only a reference style is shown. "There are two systems for citing literature in common use, the numbered system and the Harvard (name and date) system. Either is acceptable, but unless authors have a strong preference for the Harvard system we recommend that the numbered system be used." Abbreviations follow the *World List of Scientific Periodicals*.

Useful for its concise presentation of style and its discussion of scientific symbols.

31. Praeger Publishers. *Guide to manuscript preparation.* [New York?: 1978.] 38p.

"Praeger style is based on the University of Chicago's *A Manual of Style,* 12th ed., 1969."

Thirteen unnumbered sections cover basic manuscript requirements, copyediting and queries, house style, titles and heads, notes, tables and artwork, quoted material, special characteristics and mathematics, lists, front matter, back matter, permissions, and copyrights. Appendix A, "Detailed Style Characteristics," includes names of countries, adjective versus noun, word usage, abbreviations, numbers, dates, capitalization, hyphenization, hyphens versus dashes, and punctuation. Appendix B contains a short note on nondiscriminatory language. Appendix C is for authors responding to queries. No index is provided.

Bibliographic style: follows *The Chicago Manual of Style*.

32. Prentice-Hall, Inc. *Author's guide.* [5th ed., rev.] Englewood Cliffs, NJ: [1978]. x, 115p. illus. ISBN 0-13-695015-9; LC card 74-22145. (Earlier editions issued in 1937, 1952, 1955, 1957, 1960, and 1962; 5th ed. 1975.) Bibliography: p. 64.

Divided into 6 sections: preparation of the manuscript, illustrations, the technical manuscript, editing and producing the book, revisions, and supplementary teaching aids. Indexed.

Bibliographic style: unique, using small capital letters for all elements of the author's name. Commas are used between all parts of the entry.

A well-designed manual that is easy to use because of blue highlighting and its detailed index.

33. Rawson, Wade Publishers. *How to prepare a manuscript.* New York: [197–]. 13p. Photocopy.

> Contains 12 sections: typing the manuscript, corrections, contents of the manuscript, tables, illustrations and captions, footnotes, bibliographies and reference lists, glossaries and list of abbreviations, correlating parts of a manuscript, rights and permissions, material requiring permission, and how to ask permission.

> Bibliographic style: "Each item in a bibliographical list should begin flush left, . . ." with runover lines indented 3 spaces. "Authors' names in alphabetical order are typed last name first. If several works by the same author are listed, a dash (3 or 4 typed hyphens) is used in place of the author's name for each item following the first." Otherwise, only footnote style is given.

34. Rigby Limited. *Recommended Rigby style.* [Norwood, South Australia: 197–.] 5 leaves.

> Includes sections on Australian spelling, capitals, punctuation, quotation marks, ellipsis, abbreviations, numbers, quantities, dates, currency, metrication, and a list of Australian nouns and place names.

> Bibliographic style: no bibliographic style is presented.

35. Routledge & Kegan Paul. *The preparation of your typescript.* [London: 1973.] 8p.

> Divided into 8 parts: the typescript, the text, detailed points of style, notes, bibliography, index, illustrations, and permissions. No index is provided.

> Bibliographic style: title in italics, followed by publisher, place of publication, and date, all separated by commas. The Harvard system is presented as an alternative. No citations for periodical articles are given.

> Routledge & Kegan Paul also issue *Your Illustrations: Some Notes of Guidance for Our Authors* (7p.).

36. Simon and Schuster. *Author's manual.* [New York]: 1979. 15p.

> Divided into 8 parts: manuscript length; the final typescript; house style; illustrations; photographs; copyright and permissions; libel; invasion of privacy; and reading galleys. House style follows both *Words into Type* and *The Chicago Manual of Style.*

> Bibliographic style: no bibliographic style is presented.

37. Skillin, Marjorie E., Robert M. Gay, et al. *Words into type.* 3rd ed., completely rev. Englewood Cliffs, NJ: Prentice-Hall, [c1974]. xx, 585p. ISBN 0-13-964262-5; LC card 73-21726. $20.95. Includes bibliographies.

Divided into 7 parts: manuscript, copy and proof, copy-editing style, typographical style, grammar, use of words, and typography and illustration. More of an editor's and printer's manual than a writer's manual. Mathematic and scientific writing is dealt with from only the printer's point of view. Thorough treatment of word usage with long lists of trite expressions, appropriate terms, the right preposition, and words likely to be misused or confused. A good glossary of printing and allied terms (pp. 535–47) is provided. The style for some foreign languages is borrowed from the *Style Manual* (*see* item 52) issued by the Government Printing Office of the United States.

Bibliographic style: treated in 2 areas, manuscripts (pp. 37–43) and typographical style (pp. 266–69). Follows *The Chicago Manual of Style*. No reference is made to nonbook materials such as microfilms, computer tapes, films, etc.

Words into type is a useful reference work especially for editors and printers.

38. South-western Publishing Co. Editorial Department. *A style guide for authors and editors.* Cincinnati, OH: [c1970]. vi, 74p. forms. LC card 76-113431. (Not available from the publisher; available only by interlibrary loan from the Library of Congress where the call number is PN147.S64.)

Extensively illustrated guide to the writing and editorial correcting of manuscripts for a publisher of economic and business textbooks. Divided into 8 parts: 1. preparing to write, 2. manuscript format, 3. illustrative materials, 4. permissions to quote, 5. end-of-chapter and manual materials, 6. achieving final-draft manuscript, 7. proof procedures, and 8. author-publisher relationships. There are appendixes of proofreader's marks, a glossary of book-production terms, and footnote and bibliography entries. Indexed.

Bibliographic style: advocates the use of Latin abbreviations, now abandoned by Turabian and others. Appendix C. (pp. 65–71) contains numerous examples for books, for government publications, for articles in yearbooks, periodicals, encyclopedias, and newspapers and for unpublished materials. The bibliographical style is unique.

The examples of release forms for borrowed material might be of value to anyone working on textbooks.

39. Stein and Day Publishers. *Stein and Day guide for copyeditors and proofreaders.* Briarcliff Manor, NY: [197–]. 6p.

Contains short passages on punctuation, italics, numbers, abbreviations, and proofreading. For all other points of style, instructions are to "follow the University of Chicago's *A Manual of Style* except for a few house style points. . . ."

Stein and Day also has a manual on *Index Style* (1p., photocopy) and *Instructions for Manuscript Typists* (3 leaves, photocopy).

Bibliographic style: no bibliographic style is presented.

40. Thomas, Payne E. L. *A guide for authors: Manuscript, proof and illustration.* 2nd ed., rev. Springfield, IL: Thomas, [1975]. vii, 83, [1]p. illus. ISBN 0-398-03443-5; LC card 75-319945. $5.25. (First ed. 1949–65; 2nd ed. 1968–.) Bibliography: p. 77.

Divided into 10 chapters: I. considerations in writing, II. illustration selection and form, III. lettering and labeling, IV. line illustration, V. halftone illustration, VI. color illustration, VII. the final draft, VIII. proof, IX. indexing, and X. book revision. Indexed.

Bibliographic style: for books, author's full name, last name first; colon; title in italic capitals; comma; edition (if one); place; and publisher and date separated by commas. For periodical articles, author's full name, last name first; title of the article in lower case except for initial and proper nouns; name of the periodical abbreviated according to *Index Medicus* or written out in full; comma; volume number in italics; pages; comma; and year of publication. This style does not conform to the *Uniform Requirements for Manuscripts Submitted to Biomedical Journals*.

A useful manual, especially for the amount of space and detail devoted to illustrations.

41. University Publishers. Editorial Department. *Guide for authors in the preparation of manuscripts and illustrations.* Jullundur City [India: 197–?]. 42p. (Preface by O. P. Ghai.)

Divided into 18 parts: preliminary preparation, physical side, two drafts, points to remember, markings, revision, author's copy of manuscript, illustrations, front matter, back matter, punctuation, capitalization, abbreviations, spelling, usage, for author's special attention, proofreading, and some other symbols.

Bibliographic style: no bibliographic style is presented.

42. Van Nostrand Reinhold Co. *Guide for authors.* [New York: 197–.] 22p.

Covers 14 topics: the manuscript; typing of the manuscript; numbering the manuscript; penalty copy (for manuscript and illustrations); illustrations; tables; references; permissions and acknowledgments; spelling, abbreviations, and numerals; mathematical formulas; chemical formulas and equations; index; galley and page proofs; and author alterations. The booklet concludes with 4 pages of symbols and abbreviations.

Bibliographic style: examples given under "References" generally follow *The Chicago Manual of Style.*

The sections on typing the manuscript and on illustrations are well done.

43. West Publishing Co., St. Paul. *Manual for manuscript preparation: How to prepare the manuscript, how to handle the quotations, how to prepare the illustrations, how to handle citations, how to read proofs, how to make an index.* 2nd ed. St. Paul, MN: 1977. vi, 116p. ("For exclusive use of West Publishing Co. authors.")

"This manual on manuscript preparation has been prepared by the West Publishing Company to assist authors in preparing law school casebooks, student texts and other law school and college publications. . . ."

"This manuscript preparation manual includes numerous illustrations of acceptable procedures for preparing casebooks, hornbooks or textbooks, nutshells, instructor's manuals and supplements of various types for publication. It shows forms for footnotes, case citation, statute citation, titles, subtitles and names. It contains specimen pages of manuscript and many other matters." Divided into 4 chapters: 1. some preliminary instructions, which specify on what the author is to provide and what West Publishing will provide, such as a table of cases with "titles of all principal cases appearing in your casebook," 2. manuscript preparation, which covers footnotes and includes extensive illustrated pages of how new casebooks are prepared, 3. index preparation, and 4. procedures for examining galley proofs and page proofs. A long appendix provides preferred citation forms for U.S. federal and state cases and statutory materials. The volume concludes with a short index.

Bibliographic style: no bibliographic style is presented outside that mentioned above in the appendix, which provides abbreviated citations "by state showing the preferred case and statutory citation form for each state" and the format for the federal statutes, rules, and court cases.

This manual is very detailed and well illustrated concerning the preparation of new casebooks, handbooks, their supplements, and indexes. The restriction of this manual to house use prohibits its adoption by other institutions interested in legal style.

44. Wiley (John) and Sons, Inc. *A guide for Wiley authors.* New York; Chichester: [c1980]. 60p. ISBN 0-471-08373-9; LC card 80-36783. (Originally published in 1924 with title: *The manuscript, a guide for its preparation;* edition for 1973 published under title: *A guide for Wiley authors in the preparation of manuscript[s] and illustrations.* On cover: College Editing Department.)

Divided into 14 chapters: 1. instructions for the typist, 2. author's checklist, 3. writing the manuscript—the help we will give, 4. illustrations, 5. tables, 6. anthologies and reprinted material, 7. permissions procedure, 8. penalty copy, 9. author's alterations to proofs, 10. equal treatment of both sexes, 11. front matter, 12. the index, 13. Wiley staff, and 14. the production process. Indexed.

Bibliographic style: "Type double spaced, with three lines of space left between each reference. Keep references in strict alphabetical or numerical order. Based on the author's instructions, type all references throughout the manuscript in the same form and sequence. Type the cited author's given name/initial and last name consistently in either inverted or natural order. Underline book titles and journal titles (either abbreviated or written in full) to indicate italic type. Find out whether chapter and journal-article titles are to be placed in quotation marks. Give journal volume, issue, page numbers, and year of publication in the same form throughout."

The Wiley guide is a very well-designed booklet that presents the publishers admonitions to the writer in a gentle suggestive manner. It includes permission forms.

45. Wiley (John) and Sons, Inc. *A guide for Wiley-Interscience and Ronald Press authors in the preparation and production of manuscript and illustrations.* 2nd ed. New York; Chichester: [1979]. xiv, 134p. illus. ISBN 0-471-03864-4; LC card 78-24216; £5.90. ("A Wiley-Interscience Publication.") (First edition published in 1974 with title: *A guide for Wiley-Interscience authors in the preparation and production of manuscript and illustrations.*) Bibliography: pp. 115–17.

Divided into 13 parts: 1. preparation of the master manuscript, 2. illustrations and camera-ready material, 3. front matter, 4. the index, 5. writing the manuscript, 6. clear and unclear usage of grammar, 7. author's alterations to proofs, 8. multiauthor and series books, 9. new editions, books of reading, and anthologies, 10. copyright and permissions, 11. check list, 12. preview of the production process, and 13. the Wiley staff. There follow 3 appendixes: 1. copyeditor's and proofreader's marks, 2. author's reference shelf, and 3. most commonly used typographical terms. A detailed index concludes the manual.

Bibliographic style: unique style in both science and social science examples for books, chapters, periodical articles, serials, and unpublished works. Wiley accepts any alternate bibliographic or footnote style as long as it is consistent.

This manual is very useful. It provides a comprehensive overview of the entire publishing process and makes clear the role the author is to play. Especially useful are the sections on units of measure, the treatment of mathematical and chemical material, and the use of proofreader's marks for making changes in the scientific manuscript.

Wiley-Interscience and Ronald Press produce "professional and reference books and textbooks for upper-level and graduate courses and for continuing education." Interscience was originally a publisher in the field of analytical chemistry while Ronald Press was well known for its books on accounting and business.

46. York Press. *Style manual for writing & typing of scholarly works and research papers.* [Fredericton, New Brunswick: 1978.] Pamphlet (18p.) ISBN 0-919966-09-8. C$1.50.

Divided into unnumbered paragraphs of which the following are the partial contents: paper, spacing, margins, quotations, pagination, spelling, underlining, punctuation, parentheses, numerals, proofreading, title, abstract, introduction, body of the text, titles of chapters, bibliographical citations, footnotes, endnotes, abbreviations, and proofreading symbols. The index is detailed.

Bibliographic style: generally follows the style in the *MLA Handbook for Writers of Research Papers, Theses, and Dissertations.* Provides 27 examples of bibliographical citations for books and periodical articles.

GOVERNMENT PRINTING

Federal

47. Canada. Government Specifications Board. Committee on Style Manual. *Government of Canada style manual for writers and editors.* Ottawa: R. Duhamel, Queen's Printer, 1962. ix, 186p. illus. LC card 65-1317. (Cover title: *Canadian Government style manual for writers and editors.*)

"Replaces an earlier manual bearing the title: *Canadian Government Editorial Style Manual,* which was first published in 1939," by the Government Purchasing Standards Committee. " . . . out of print . . . a revised English edition should be available at the end of 1984" (letter to the compiler dated March 9, 1983).

Divided into 20 sections: organization and prose style, grammar, the preparation of copy, abbreviations, capital letters, compounding of words, headings, italics, numerical expressions, punctuation, quotations, reference matter, spelling, graphic presentation, tabular presentation, illustrations, reading and correction of proofs, make-up of a book, glossary of printing terms, and an appendix of the Greek alphabet and astronomical and mathematical signs. The index is good.

Bibliographic style: covered in detail in the chapter on reference matter. Not unlike that presented on Library of Congress printed cards. Numerous examples for multiauthored books, corporate authors, translations, transliterations, etc. For periodical articles, journal titles are abbreviated according to the *International Code for the Abbreviation of Titles of Periodicals* and the *World List of Scientific Periodicals*. The date of the article follows its pagination.

Useful, detailed manual. Especially good on illustrative matter. Comprehensive, but now somewhat out of date.

48. India. Ministry of Information and Broadcasting. Publications Division. *Publications Division style book.* [New Delhi: ca. 1973.] 20p.

". . . . a cyclostyled style sheet which has been prepared for the editorial staff of the Publications Division. This may kindly be treated as the style sheet of the Publications Division only and not of the government of India. To our knowledge, there is no Government of India style manual as such."

Divided into 14 sections: contents of a manuscript, quotated [*sic*] matter, dates and numbers, numbers, use of capitals, division of a word, abbreviations, italics, spellings, hyphens, agreement between subject and verb, punctuation, references, and appendix.

Bibliographic style: unique. Major elements separated by commas, with price added at end. Periodical articles use ''in'' before italicized periodical title, then follow place of publication, date, and pagination, all separated by commas.

49. New Zealand. Government Printing Office. *Style book: A guide addressed to all writers, editors, and public servants who prepare manuscripts for publication by the Government Printing Office.* 3rd ed. Wellington: P. D. Hasselberg, Government Printer, 1981. 255p. ISBN 0-477-01118-7. (First ed. 1958; 2nd ed. 1968.)

> Divided into 14 chapters: 1. preparing copy, 2. italics, 3. punctuation, 4. capitals, 5. spelling, 6. division of words, 7. compound words, 8. numbers, 9. abbreviations, 10. animals and plants: their common names and diseases and pests, 11. common errors and pitfalls: a guide to correct usage, 12. official section: Parliamentary papers, regulations, *New Zealand Gazette,* bills, and order papers, 13. metrication, and 14. a glossary of printing terms. The volume has a detailed index.

> Bibliographic style: no bibliographic style is presented.

> ''This new edition incorporates further amendments; the chapters dealing with the preparation of copy, abbreviations, and compound words have been revised; new material has been added to the chapters dealing with the common names of animals and plants, errors in the use of English in official writing, and terms used in printing. The introduction of metrication has required a new chapter as well as amendments throughout the book.'' The New Zealand government *Style Book* is useful for its list of indigenous plants and animals and for its detailed treatment of official publications of the New Zealand government.

50. Pitson, John. *Style manual for authors, editors and printers of Australian government publications.* 3rd ed. Revised by John Pitson. Canberra: Australian Government Publishing Service, 1978. xvi, 463p. illus. ISBN 0-642-033463 case bound, ISBN 0-642-033455 pbk. A$8.00pbk. (First ed. 1966; 2nd ed. 1972.) Bibliography: pp. 415–17.

> Divided into 5 major parts: writing and editing, copy and proofs, designing for print, printing, and duplicating and copying. In turn, the 5 major topics are subdivided into 29 chapters: 1. writing, 2. spelling, 3. capitals, 4. italics, 5. punctuation, 6. quotations, 7. abbreviations and contractions, 8. numbers, dates and currency, 9. units of measurement, 10. notes, references and bibliographies, 11. indexing, 12. preparing copy, 13. standing matter, 14. correcting proofs, 15. typography, 16. type faces, 17. format, 18. the parts of a publication, 19.

paper, 20. illustrations, 21. maps, 22. heraldic and other devices, 23. typographical style rules, 24. dividing words, 25. make-up and imposition, 26. typesetting and printing processes, 27. binding, 28. duplicating, copying and microfilming, and 29. typing for reproduction. The volume also includes 11 appendixes: I. honorifics and modes of address, II. the law relating to publication, III. difficult spellings, IV. forms, V. foreign alphabets, VI. mathematics, science and music, VII. special signs and symbols, VIII. foreign currencies, IX. paper sizes, X. standard page dimensions, and XI. metric conversion tables. There follow a glossary (pp. 419–36) and a detailed index.

Bibliographic style: Author's name in small capitals, title of book in italics (proper nouns and initial word capitalized), edition statement, publisher, place of publication, and date. A periodical article title has single quotes. The title of the periodical is in italics (proper nouns and initial words are capitalized). There follow the volume number in roman, comma, issue number in roman, comma, and month and year separated from inclusive pages by a comma.

For a review of the section of indexing (pp. 104–11) *see* L. M. Harrod, "Style Manual for Authors, Editors and Printers of Australian Government Publications," *The Indexer* 11 (Oct. 1979): 232–34. This manual is the best designed and best illustrated of all the government style manuals. It is also the best integrated manual, with one topic flowing naturally into the next. It includes a good explanation of the Harvard footnote citation system. It is weak on foreign alphabets (cf. *Style Manual* of the Government Printing Office of the United States, item 52). The manual's strengths are its typography, illustrations, honorifics, and the treatment of Australian government documents.

51. Rhodesia. Department of Printing and Stationery. *Manual of style for the drafting and preparation of copy*. Salisbury: Government Printer, [1978]. iii, 20p. (Foreword by L. G. Smith; preface by Harry W. H. Read.)

Divided into 32 unnumbered sections: preparation and submission of printer's copy; Oxford spelling; words frequently spelt incorrectly; the correct use of initial capitals; commas; colons and semicolons; the use of the apostrophe; quotation marks; parentheses, brackets and dashes; the use of the hyphen; printing of numbers; metric symbols; descriptions of areas; reference marks; words which cannot be qualified; division of words; printing of addresses; abbreviations and symbols; years with A.D. or B.C.; continuation lines; initials and letters of distinction; ellipses; repeating the same meaning; collective nouns; explanatory notes; allegoric and metaphoric phraseology; tedious repetition of favorite words; changing from singular to plural; choice of words; reprinting of forms; special requirements for lithography, and the index.

Bibliographic style: no bibliographic style is presented.

The section on "Words Frequently Spelt Incorrectly" is useful for some Zimbabwean place names.

52. United States. Government Printing Office. *Style manual.* Rev. ed. Washington, DC: For sale by the Superintendent of Documents, USGPO, 1973. viii, 548p. LC card 72-600382. $4.25. (Title varies: 1894–1909, *Manual of style;* 1911–17, *Style book.)* (Edition statements inconsistent.) (Abridged editions: 1933, 1939, 1945, 1953, 1959, 1967.)

Divided into 25 chapters covering the following topics: 1. suggestions to authors and editors, 2. general instructions, 3. capitalization, 4. guide to capitalization, 5. spelling, 6. compound words, 7. guide to compounding, 8. punctuation, 9. abbreviations, 10. signs and symbols, 11. italic, 12. numerals, 13. tabular work, 14. leaderwork, 15. text footnotes, indexes, and contents, 16. datelines, addresses, and signatures, 17. courtwork, 18. useful tables, 19. counties, 20. plant and insect names, 21. patents, 22. Congressional Record, 23. Senate and House journals, 24. nominations, reports, documents, laws, and 25. foreign languages: Danish, Dutch, Finnish, French, German, Greek (classical and modern), Hebrew, Hungarian, Italian, Latin, Norwegian, Polish, Portuguese, Russian, Spanish, Swedish, Turkish, and Slavic languages and their alphabets. Detailed index.

Bibliographic style: although 2 examples of a bibliographic style are given for United States government documents (p. 9), the material presented is too brief to stand as a bibliographic statement. Both examples have unique formats not found elsewhere among the major style manuals.

Although primarily a printer's manual, the GPO *Style Manual* is also an invaluable reference tool for the writer. It is especially good for its detailed discussion of word division, its examples of tabular material, its abbreviations, its words of Latin origin, and its section on patents. It is best known for its typography of foreign languages.

In 1934, the Government Printing Office issued *Foreign Languages for the Use of Printers and Translators,* which is currently available from Boardman, Clark Co., New York, under the title: *Manual of Foreign Languages for the Use of Librarians, Bibliographers, Research Workers, Editors, Translators, and Printers,* by George F. von

Ostermann (4th ed., rev. and enl., 1952 [1970], 414p., $25.00). *See also Hart's Rules for Compositors and Readers at the University Press, Oxford* (item 106) for another presentation of rules for the typography of foreign languages.

State

53. California. Office of State Printing. *Style and procedure.* [Prepared by members of the proofroom staff.] Sacramento, CA: 1976. 61p. illus.

"Section 14854 of the Government Code provides that the Office of State Printing shall decide upon the style and manner of printing all laws and other state documents except those printed for the legislature."

Divided into 3 major parts: suggestions to authors, instructions to printers, and general information. Suggestions to authors covers printing style, copy form and preparation, photographs and other art, requisition of printing, printing services, proofreading, and preparing dummy. Instructions to printers treat abbreviations, blanks, briefs, capitalization, closemark, imprint, runline, communications, compounding, directories, division, figures, footnotes, reference marks, scientific works, spelling, tables, composition, dump bank, correction blank, make-up, copyholding, and proofreading. General information covers spelling, geographical abbreviations, the Greek alphabet, the metric system, the pledge to the flag, signatures, basic stock sizes, type measurement, photoelectric composition, parahomonyms and anagrams, heterosyllabic homographs, copyreaders' marks, copy preparation symbols, and proofreaders' marks.

Bibliographic style: no bibliographic style is presented.

Author section of the manual is primarily devoted to illustration. Good printers' manual with a long list of California place names, parahomonyms and anagrams, and heterosyllabic homographs.

54. Kansas. State Department of Social and Rehabilitation Services. *Style manual.* Topeka, KS: 1976. 47p. (loose-leaf) with 3 punched holes for a ring binder. (1963 edition issued by State Department of Social Welfare of Kansas.)

"This manual has been developed as a guide for the clerical staff of the State Department of Social and Rehabilitation Services to use in their day-to-day job." Divided into 14 parts: preface, general, letters and envelopes, titles and proper addresses, capitalization, punctuation, grammar, spelling, syllabication, abbreviations, numbers and figures, setting up material in outline form, filing, and telephone techniques.

Bibliographic style: no bibliographic style is presented.

55. Kansas. State Printer. *Type and style.* Topeka, KS: 1954. 78p. illus.

"These rules serve as a guide for the linotype operators and proofreaders at the State Printing Plant." Divided into 2 main sections: style manual and specimens of type. The former treats capitalization, the use of italics, abbreviations, the Supreme Court, numbers, money, a few words and forms, headings, index work, brief work, school catalogues, general style, tabular matter, and proofreaders' marks. The latter, specimens of type, forms the bulk of the manual. Red ink is used effectively to highlight the type and to decorate the manual.

Bibliographic style: no bibliographic style is presented.

56. New South Wales. Government Printing Office. *Printing style manual.* Ultimo: 1970. [Rev. ed. 1969.] x, 348p. A$2.25, prepay plus postage ca. A$2.40 surface mail to North America. (First ed. 1966; new ed. in preparation.)

Includes 17 chapters: 1. suggestions to authors and editors, 2. general instructions, 3. capitalization, 4. spelling, 5. compound and derived words, 6. punctuation, 7. numericals, 8. abbreviations and contractions, 9. signs and symbols, 10. italic, 11. tabular work, 12. footnotes, indexes, and contents, 13. bills and acts, 14. *Parliamentary Debates (Hansard),* 15. courtwork-appeal books, 16. foreign words and phrases, and 17. useful information. Detailed index.

Bibliographic style: no bibliographic style is presented.

Much of this style manual is derived from the *Style Manual* of the United States Government Printing Office *(see* item 52), which is not copyrighted. Permission to borrow from the USGPO was granted, and most of the New South Wales style manual reproduces sentences or sections verbatim. Only "plants and insect names" in the USGPO style manual was omitted. The treatment of the government documents of New South Wales is unique.

57. New York (State). Division of the Budget. *Style manual.* [Albany?, NY: 1973.] 44p.

"This Style Manual is for use by all Budget Division staff in preparing materials for the annual Budget document and other official reports. . . . The Manual was prepared by Josephine Braden, under the direction of George Von Frank."

Divided into 15 parts: effective writing, abbreviations, capitalization, compound words and hyphens, correspondence, dates, lists and enumerations, numbers, plurals and singulars, prepositions, punctuation, spelling, tables, words commonly misused or misplaced, and references. Indexed.

Bibliographic style: no bibliographic style is presented.

TERM PAPERS AND THESES

58. Allen, Eliot D., and Ethel B. Colbrunn. *A short guide to writing a research paper, manuscript form, and documentation.* Rev. ed. Deland, FL: Everett/Edwards, [1978]. iv, 35, 6p. ISBN 0-912112-19-0. $2.50. (1963 edition with title: *A short guide to manuscript form and documentation.*) Includes sample bibliographies.

"This manual has been revised to comply with the second edition of *The MLA Style Sheet.*" Divided into 2 major parts: the first, writing a research paper, including sections on choosing a subject, using the library, note-taking, making an outline, and writing the paper, and a second part entitled manuscript form and documentation, which covers paper, margins, pagination, paragraph indentation, title, quotations, plagiarism, footnotes, footnote and bibliography form for papers in the humanities, social sciences, and sciences, abbreviations, and a sample outline with a sample research paper.

Bibliographic style: presents a style not unlike that represented in the *MLA Handbook for Writers of Research Papers, Theses, and Dissertations,* except that italics are omitted. Separate sample forms are given for biology, geology, psychology, chemistry, and mathematics. These latter are all variants of Harvard style. Authors are advised to consult the style manual of their respective sciences.

59. Allen, Eliot D., and Ethel B. Colbrunn. *The student writer's guide.* Rev. ed. Deland, FL: Everett/Edwards, [1976, c1970]. vii, 176p. forms. ISBN 0-912112-18-2; LC card 77-89571. $5.00.

"*The Student Writer's Guide* is intended to be used as a textbook in composition classes and as a reference book for the individual student." This guide originated in the English Department of Stetson University. "This manual has been revised to conform with the second edition of *The MLA Style Sheet.*"

Divided into 9 parts: preface; writing themes; writing research papers; writing critical reviews; paragraphs; sentences; usage; punctuation, miscellaneous mechanics and manuscript form; and exercises.

Bibliographic style: Modern Language Association of America's *The MLA Style Sheet,* 2nd ed. (now superseded by the association's *MLA Handbook*). Includes examples and explanations of footnotes and bibliography.

60. Allen, George R. *The graduate students' guide to theses and dissertations: A practical manual for writing and research.* San Francisco, CA: Jossey-Bass, 1974. xi, 108p. ISBN 0-87589-182-9; LC card 73-3774. $10.95. Bibliography: pp. 97–105.

> Divided into 7 chapters: 1. academic research, 2. selecting the research topic, 3. research committee, 4. research proposal, 5. data collection and analysis, 6. writing the research report, and 7. dissertation defense. A set of questions is provided for each of chapters 1-7. The work concludes with a short index.
>
> Bibliographic style: no bibliographic style is presented.
>
> Very readable manual that might serve as background and introduction to the major style manuals, it provides few details and presents no overall style.

61. Anderson, Jonathan, Berry H. Durston, and Millicent Poole. *Thesis and assignment writing.* Sydney; New York: Wiley, [1970]. xi, 135p. ISBN 0-471-02901-7, ISBN 0-471-02899-1pbk.; LC card 72-132006. Out of print. Bibliography: p. 122.

> Three major parts: I. assignments and theses at the tertiary level, II. writing the thesis or assignment, and III. revising the assignment or thesis. Within the 3 parts are 12 chapters: 1. writing at the tertiary level, 2. planning the assignment, 3. planning the thesis, 4. scholarly writing: a case study, 5. the general format, 6. page and chapter format, 7. the use of quotations, 8. footnotes, 9. tables and figures, 10. referencing, 11. appendixes, and 12. editing and evaluating the final product. There follow a list of useful references and an appendix entitled "Meanings and Examples of Abbreviations Commonly Used in Assignments and Theses." Indexed.
>
> Bibliographic style: Harvard. Examples are provided for books, periodical articles, edited works, translations, anonymous and pseudonymous publications, conference proceedings, corporate entries, unpublished materials, and theses.

"This book is designed to provide practical help and guidance to students at the tertiary level in their writing of essays, assignments, tutorial papers, reports, theses and dissertations. It should prove useful to both undergraduate and post graduate students." The material is concisely presented and perhaps half the manual is filled with examples. A useful manual that suggests rather than prescribes answers to questions of style.

62. Anderson, Kenneth E., and Oscar M. Haugh. *A handbook for the preparation of research reports and theses*. [Washington, DC]: University Press of America, [c1978]. iv, 43p. ports. ISBN 0-8191-0597-4; LC card 78-61395. $5.00.

"The present handbook has been prepared to aid graduate students in Education to resolve some of the most common problems confronting the writer of a research report." Divided into 3 major parts: general organization of the report, technical and mechanical problems of thesis writing—including style of writing, spelling, foreign words and phrases, capitalization, punctuation, pagination, chapter title and subdivision headings, series entries and listings, use of numbers in context, formulas, margins and spacing, quotations, numbering of footnotes, footnote form, form for bibliographical entries, and tabular and illustrative materials—and appendixes of sample pages, comprising more than half the book.

Bibliographic style: presented only in Appendix E as a sample bibliography of books, periodical articles, general reference books, bulletins, and unpublished material. Style for books is unique, with full name of publisher coming before place of publication. Style for periodical articles is almost identical to that presented in *The Chicago Manual of Style*. Useful for its extended appendixes containing sample pages of title pages, acknowledgment page, table of contents, list of tables, bibliographic forms, chapter title and subdivision headings, quotations and ellipses, and suggestions to the typist.

63. Auckland University Press. *The preparation and style of manuscripts*. 3rd ed. [Auckland?: 1977, c1964.] 26p. [First edition (1964) and 2nd edition (1965) have title: *Notes on the preparation and style of manuscripts.*] Bibliography: pp. 25–26.

"In their original version, the notes followed the order and decisions of the 'MLA Style Sheet', *Publications of the Modern Language Association*, v. 56, April 1951, pp. 3–31, with some changes chiefly in the interests of simplicity and consistency." Divided into 11 sections: introduction, thesis and book, preparing the typescript, the text, documentation, abbreviations and reference words, bibliography, the Harvard system, index, correcting proof, and an appendix for writers of theses. Footnote citations are dealt with in some detail with an interesting discussion of the Harvard system.

Bibliographic style: for a book, there are 4 elements: author, title in italics, place of publication, and date of publication. Periodical articles include author; title in italics, in single quotes, and abbreviated according to the forms in the *Draft British Standard Specifications for the Abbreviations of Titles of Periodicals* (1971); volume number; date; and inclusive paging.

Valuable for its insight into the relationship between a thesis and a published book.

64. Berry, Dorothea M., and Gordon P. Martin. *A guide to writing research papers*. New York: McGraw-Hill, [1972, c1971]. viii, 161p. ISBN 0-07-005029-5,SP; LC card 70-139549. $2.95. Bibliography: pp. 123–52.

''*A Guide to Writing Research Papers* is a thorough revision and expansion of earlier editions issued in mimeographed form by the Bookstore of the University of California, Riverside, in 1956 and 1959.'' Divided into 6 chapters: I. organization and writing of the paper, II. theses and dissertations, III. documentation, IV. tables and illustrations, V. scientific papers, and VI. typing the manuscript. The appendix, entitled research methods and sources, has 5 sections: A. selecting a subject, B. sources of information, C. reference works, D. outline, and E. note-taking. Indexed.

Bibliographic style: follows *The Chicago Manual of Style,* except for numbers of periodical volumes where Berry and Martin use roman numerals in place of arabic ones. Citations for biology and chemistry are out of date because editors in these fields have adopted the *American National Standard for Bibliographic References.*

The material is presented in outline format with examples. The guide is written for ''the problems and questions of undergraduate students writing term papers, of graduate students writing theses and dissertations, of faculty members preparing manuscripts for publication, and of their typists.''

65. Berry, Ralph. *How to write a research paper*. New York: Pergamon, [1969]. 121p. ISBN 0-08-006423-X, ISBN 0-08-006392-6pbk.; LC card 69-17176. $5.50pbk.

Divided into 7 chapters: I. the choice of subject: using the library, II. preparing a bibliography, III. taking notes, IV. composing the paper, V. the final version, VI. specimen paper, and VII. some errors to avoid. No index is provided.

Bibliographic style: recommends *The MLA Style Sheet*, first edition, which was superseded in 1970 by the second edition and in 1977 by the *MLA Handbook for Writers of Research Papers, Theses, and Dissertations*. The volume includes very few examples.

A short manual "designed to be relevant from the senior grade through the various states of college education." A large part of the manual is devoted to a "specimen paper" (pp. 77–112). Instructions are sometimes confusing. Explanations are not provided with the prescripts.

66. Campbell, William G., Stephen V. Ballou, and Carole Slade. *Form and style: Theses, reports, term papers*. 6th ed. Boston: Houghton Mifflin [c1982, 1978]. x, 210p.   ISBN 0-395-31689-8; LC card 81-82571; $8.95pbk. [First edition (1939) has title: *A form for thesis writing*. 2nd ed. 1954; 3rd ed. 1969; 4th ed. 1974; 5th ed. 1978].

Divided into 8 parts: 1. writing research papers, 2. elements of theses and dissertations, 3. quotations, 4. notes: footnotes and endnotes, 5. bibliographies, 6. tables, figures, and computer materials, 7. style and mechanics, and 8. the final paper. There is a brief glossary of special terms and abbreviations followed by an index.

This manual is laid out "as a basic text in writing courses at many levels and as a supplementary text for any course that requires the writing of research papers or term papers." There is an in-depth discussion of footnotes and endnotes with numerous examples.

Bibliographic style: presents both the style of the *MLA Handbook for Writers of Research Papers, Theses, and Dissertations* and *The Chicago Manual of Style*. Sample pages of bibliographies are provided including those with annotations and those employing "references-cited format" such as author-year format, also called Harvard style, and author-number format. There are pages of examples for journals, magazines, newspapers, reviews, books, multivolume works and series, reference works, works of literature, government and other official documents, unpublished sources, nonprint sources, and microform materials.

This manual is explicit in its instructions, well designed, easy to use, and up to date. It is particularly recommended for its many examples that serve to clarify difficult problems in writing a research paper.

67. Council of Biology Editors. Committee on Graduate Training on Scientific Writing. *Scientific writing for graduate students; a manual on the teaching of scientific writing.* Edited by F. Peter Woodford. [Arlington, VA]: Council of Biology Editors, 1981. x, 190p. $7.50. First printing 1968; reprinted 1976 and 1981. Bibliography: pp. 179–84.

Divided into 2 parts: Pt. 1, writing a journal article, by F. Peter Woodford comprises the first 9 chapters: 1. clearing away the underbrush, 2. the ground plan, 3. the master plan, 4. the first draft, 5. the first revision: structural alterations, 6. further revision: polishing the style, 7. editing assignments, 8. the final steps, and 9. responding to the editor. Pt. 2, related topics, comprises the last 5 chapters: 10. design of tables and figures, by F. Peter Woodford, 11. preparation for writing the doctoral thesis, by Edwin L. Cooper, 12. writing a research project proposal, by F. Peter Woodford, 13. oral presentation of a scientific paper, by Ellsworth B. Cook, and 14. principles and practices in searching the scientific literature, by Marcus Rosenblum. Subject and name indexes are provided.

Bibliographic style: Harvard, with examples of errors in sample papers.

The manual is designed primarily for the teacher and student of scientific writing at the graduate level. The author and editor are referred to the *Style Manual* of the Council of Biology Editors. Because sample texts and footnotes are annotated in parallel pages, the manual lends itself to textbook instruction. Useful for anyone wishing to improve his/her style because the text is written to be read through rather than formatted like a reference book. *Scientific Writing for Graduate Students* is carefully and professionally well done.

68. Coyle, William. *Research papers.* 5th ed. Indianapolis, IN: Bobbs-Merrill Educational Publishing, [1980]. x, 214p. ISBN 0-672-61500-2pbk.; LC card 79-14110. $6.95. (First ed. 1959? 2nd ed. 1965; 3rd ed. 1971; 4th ed. 1976.)

Divided into 6 topics: 1. choosing a topic, 2. using the library, 3. gathering material, 4. constructing an outline, 5. documentation, and 6. writing the paper. A short index is provided.

Bibliographic style: follows the *MLA Handbook for Writers of Research Papers, Theses, and Dissertations.* Alternative examples are provided, but their source is not documented. Out of date for some of the sciences, notably biology and chemistry, whose editors have adopted the *American National Standard for Bibliographic References.* Provides explanations and examples for bibliographic citations to books, magazines, anonymous works, anthologies, book reviews, collaborators, corporate authors, editions, editors, encyclopedias, films, illustrators, interviews, introductions, joint authorship, legal references, magazines continuously paged, manuscript materials, research papers, newspapers, pamphlets, personal letters, pseudonyms, public documents, reprints, series, subtitles, television programs, titles within titles, translations, untitled articles, volumes of a multi-volumed monograph, and works by the same author.

"This manual is designed to guide a student in preparing a research paper for a freshman writing course and also in writing term papers for other college courses." The approach is step by step with considerable discussion given to the examples presented. Exercise pages are also provided. The format is spacious, and the manual is easy to use; however, the use of variant examples throughout clearly requires an instructor's explanation.

69. Dawe, Jessamon. *Writing business and economics papers, theses, and dissertations.* Totowa, NJ: Littlefield, Adams, 1965. vii, 192p. (*A Littlefield, Adams quality paperback,* no. 96.) ISBN 0-8226-0096-Xpbk.; LC card 66-18148. $3.50.

Divided into 11 chapters: 1. the research process—an overview, 2. selecting and defining the problem, 3. building a research design, 4. data-gathering techniques, 5. organizing the outline, 6. writing the introductory chapters, 7. developing the content chapters, 8. tabular and graphic illustration, 9. drafting the conclusions and recommendations, 10. writing style for the scholarly paper, 11. make-up, format, and documentation. Some chapters include bibliographies.

Bibliographic style: for books, identical to *The Chicago Manual of Style.* For periodicals, identical to Chicago style except that roman numerals are used for volume numbers and a comma is placed before the pagination. Includes examples for public documents, reports, and unpublished theses and laws.

Dawe' step-by-step approach creates a manual that is easy to follow.

70. Dugdale, Kathleen. *A manual of form for theses and term papers.* 5th ed. Bloomington, IN: [For sale by the Indiana University Bookstore, Business Office, c1972]. 59p. illus. ISBN 0-9600028-2-0. $4.00 plus $1.50 for postage and packing. (1950 edition has title: *A manual of form for theses and term papers, designed for authors and typists;* rev. eds. 1955 and 1962; 3rd ed. 1967.)

Divided into 7 unnumbered parts: mechanical detail♥, suggestions concerning the writing of the study, general typographical form, preliminary pages, special types of material in text, supplementary pages, and final suggestions. Indexed.

Bibliographic style: unique. Uses commas to separate all elements with italics reserved for titles. Citations for government documents differ markedly from the styles of the major style manuals.

71. Durrenberger, Robert W. *Geographical research and writing*. New York: Crowell, [c1971]. ix, 246p. illus. ISBN 0-690-32301-8; LC card 77-136033. Out of print.

" . . . developed as a guide to assist students doing research and writing in the field of geography. Although directed specifically to undergraduates preparing their first research papers in geography courses, it will also be useful to students doing advanced work in the field." It is divided into 2 major parts. Research and writing includes information on the nature of geographical research, identifying a problem and developing a research plan, research methods, and preparing the manuscript, with appendixes on "The Four Traditions of Geography," by William D. Pattison, the editorial policy and style sheet of the *Annals* of the Association of American Geographers, and a list of the volumes of *The Professional Geographer* containing dissertations and theses on geographical topics. The second half, aids to geographical research, "supplements and updates John K. Wright and Elizabeth Platt's Aid to Geographical Research, 2nd ed." and includes bibliographies of general guides, bibliographies and sources of information, special indexes, abstracts, and bibliographies, major sources of statistical information, map sources, sources of photographs, and a selected list of periodicals used by geographers. Includes an index of geographical works cited and a subject index.

Bibliographic style: generally follows *The Chicago Manual of Style* with some minor changes in punctuation.

72. Gatner, Elliott S. M., and Francesco Cordasco. *Research and report writing*. Rev. ed. Totowa, NJ: Littlefield, Adams, 1974. vii, 146p. (*A Littlefield, Adams quality paperback, no. 277.*) ISBN 0-8226-0277-6; LC card 74-4069. $2.95. [1946 edition and 1947 edition have title: *University handbook for research and report writing:* 1948 edition has title: *Handbook for research and report writing*; 2nd edition (1951) has title: *Handbook for research writing;* other editions were published in 1955, 1956, 1958, and 1963. Revised edition of the 1963 edition was published by Barnes & Noble, New York. On earlier editions, Gatner's name appeared first on the title page. This entry follows the practice of the U.S. Library of Congress and other libraries contributing to the U.S. National Union Catalog.]

Divided into 11 chapters: I. introduction, II. the use of the library, III. the collection and organization of materials, IV. the techniques of composition, V. general works, language and literature, VI. mathematics, natural and physical sciences, VII. sociology, political science and government, law, history, VIII. economics and business, IX. psychology, education, and philosophy, X. music, theater, fine arts, and XI. specimen papers. An index is provided but in very fine print.

Bibliographic style: unique, but resembles U.S. Library of Congress card style: " . . . we have used the form preferred by most librarians (with the exception that we have purposely omitted the pagination [for books]). . . ."

"This manual is designed primarily for use by college freshmen and sophomores; but enough material has been given to make it useful throughout the remainder of the undergraduate courses, and, to a limited extent, in the early phases of graduate study." Roughly one-third of the manual is devoted to partially annotated bibliographies on the topics cited above. Another third of the manual is given over to 4 specimen papers. The remainder (the beginning) is devoted to matters of style. Students looking for comprehensive bibliographies will find some relevant items in this manual. However, many titles have been superseded by later research in the 1970s. This manual needs to be updated.

73. Gorn, Janice L. *Style guide for writers of term papers, masters' theses, and doctoral dissertations*. [New York]: Monarch Press, [c1973]. v, 107p. illus. ISBN 0-671-18789-9. $3.50. Bibliography: pp. 92–93.

Divided into 10 parts: how to take notes; usage; format; documentation through footnotes; bibliography; tables, figures, charts, graphs, and illustrations; the term paper; the doctoral dissertation and the master's thesis; foreign words and abbreviations; and foreword, acknowledgments, table of contents, and abbreviations. Appendixes include abbreviations for singular and plural forms of English and Latin nouns and sample title pages for term papers, masters' theses, dissertation proposals, and doctoral dissertations. Indexed.

Bibliographic style: for books, generally follows *The Chicago Manual of Style*. For periodical articles, the style presented is unique. The chapter on bibliography presents a sample bibliography as a model rather than prescribing style. The sequence of elements is clearly presented, but not enough explanation is provided.

A well-arranged and well-illustrated manual, formatted to present various "rules" followed by examples.

74. Helm, Ernest Eugene, and Albert T. Luper. *Words and music: Form and procedure in theses, dissertations, research papers, book reports, programs, and theses in composition.* [Hackensack, NJ: Joseph Boonin, 1971.] v, 78p. ISBN 0-913574-00-7. $5.00. Bibliography: pp. 2–4.

Divided into 5 chapters: I. theses and research papers wholly or partly typewritten, II. book formats, III. programs, IV. theses in composition, and V. some commonly broken rules of good writing. Indexed.

Bibliographic style: for books, it follows *The Chicago Manual of Style.* For periodical articles and articles in encyclopedias and dictionaries, editions of music, photocopied materials, unpublished typescripts, manuscripts and recordings, there is a unique format. Examples for other bibliographic forms are not given. Roman numerals are used for periodical volume numbering.

"This book is intended to serve as a guide for every kind of serious writing on music. It is primarily directed toward graduate and undergraduate students in colleges and universities. . . ." Many sample pages are provided throughout the manual. The bibliography needs updating.

75. Hungerford, Lynda. How to write term papers, theses, and dissertations. In *The Writer's Manual.* [Palm Springs, CA: ETC Publications, 1979.] (*The Writer's manual,* book 10 pp. 679–760.) ISBN 0-88280-087-6, ISBN 0-88280-088-4pbk.; LC card 75-43588. $27.95, $16.95pbk.

Divided into 3 parts. Part I, research and writing, includes the introduction, what must be done, libraries, the reference room, the growth of a bibliography, the card catalog, library stacks, interlibrary loan, evaluating sources, taking notes, preliminary writing, writing habits, the first draft, revision, transitions, documentation and citation, explanatory footnotes, and style. Part II, form, includes the final draft; the preliminary matter; the text; reference notes; first reference to a book, periodical, government document, unpublished material; shortening and eliminating notes; subsequent references; and checking your quotations and bibliographies. Part III, appendixes, includes sample bibliography, title pages, and tables of contents. A combined index appears at the end of the volume.

Bibliographic style: follows *The Chicago Manual of Style.*

An effective essay on style and its application, useful for anyone preparing a paper in the humanities. Easy to read with large type on a spacious page.

76. Hurt, Peyton. *Bibliography and footnotes: A style manual for students and writers.* 3rd ed., rev. and enl. by Mary L. Hurt Richmond. Berkeley, CA: University of California Press, 1968. xii, 163p. ISBN 0-520-00589-9; CALI50; LC card 67-26633. $6.95. (Editions for 1936 and 1949 have title: *Bibliography and footnotes: A style manual for college and university students.*) Bibliography: pp. 149–50.

Divided into 4 parts: bibliography, footnotes, scientific and technical references, and typing the manuscript. There follow a section of specimen pages, a selected list of references, and a detailed index.

Bibliographic style: useful for its lengthy discussion and numerous examples of government documents from the United States, individual state and municipal authorities, and the United Kingdom and the United Nations. The chapter on scientific and technical references is too short to be helpful. The use of roman numerals in citations for periodical articles is out of date.

A concise style manual, still valuable for its treatment of government documents.

77. Irvine, Demar B. *Writing about music: A style book for reports and theses.* 2nd ed., rev. and enl. Seattle, WA; London: University of Washington Press, [c1968]. xiii, 211p. ISBN 0-295-78558-6; LC Card 56-13245 $7.95. (First ed. 1956.) Bibliography: pp. 203–04.

Divided into 2 major parts: style in the typescript and writing skills. Style in the typescript includes 13 chapters: I. the draft, II. the typescript, III. titles, headings, captions, legends, IV. punctuation, V. numerals, dates, VI. spelling, foreign words, abbreviations, VII. footnote references, VIII. footnote discussion, IX. bibliography, X. references in the text, XI. illustrative material, XII. duplicating, photocopying, and printing processes, and XIII. the thesis. Writing skills contains 6 chapters: XIV. abstract, paraphrase, direct quotation, XV. organization of the paper, XVI. communication of ideas at paragraph, sentence, and word levels, XVII. control of literary style, XVIII. kinds of writing, and XIX. writing for publication. The appendix consists of a sample paper, and a detailed index is provided.

Bibliographic style: unique. In some examples, it resembles elements as arranged in *The Chicago Manual of Style.* Uses roman numerals for volume designations for both books and periodical articles. Edition statements are inconsistent in the use of arabic numbers, as opposed to spelling them out (cf. examples on pp. 84–85). Stresses annotations in bibliographies. Abbreviations are used sparingly.

Useful, but the bibliographic style is out of date.

78. Kahn, Gilbert, and Donald J. D. Mulkerne. *The term paper, step by step.* 2nd ed., rev. by Donald J. D. Mulkerne. Garden City, NY: Anchor Books, Doubleday, [c1977]. 90p. ISBN 0-385-12380-9pbk; LC card 76-16253. $3.50pbk. (Authors' names reversed on title page.) Bibliography: pp. 20–29.

Divided into 9 chapters: 1. introduction, 2. choosing and limiting the subject, 3. using the library, 4. preparing the bibliography, 5. taking notes, 6. making the outline, 7. writing the paper, 8. footnoting, and 9. typing the paper. A list of abbreviations used in reference books and a sample term paper, as well as a short index, are provided.

Bibliographic style: incomplete. Pagination is omitted in sample entries. No consistent bibliographic pattern is discernible.

Cursory examination of the elements that make up a research paper. Not enough attention is paid to discussing the problems of organization, the details of footnotes, and the elements of bibliography.

79. Lester, James D. *Writing research papers: a complete guide.* 3rd ed. Glenview, IL: Scott, Foresman and Co., [1980]. [ix], 207p. ISBN 0-673-15327-4; LC card 79-27837. $4.95. (First ed. 1967; 2nd ed. 1976.) Bibliography: pp. 168–96.

Divided into 7 chapters: 1. the preliminaries, 2. gathering data, 3. taking notes, 4. writing your paper, 5. endnotes and footnotes, 6. the bibliography, and 7. documentation of science papers. Appendix 1 is a glossary of additional research terms, while Appendix 2 is a list of general reference books and journals. A detailed index is provided.

Bibliographic style: with the exception of the science citations, Lester's guide follows the *MLA Handbook for Writers of Research Papers, Theses, and Dissertations.*

A detailed style manual designed for the college classroom. Elements other than bibliographic follow the *MLA Handbook.* Use of red color in the book's subheads and highlighting is effective; even the sample research paper is annotated in red. Many examples of both footnotes and bibliographic citations are included; however, the examples in the chapter on the "Documentation of Science Papers" have been superseded in biology and chemistry by the adoption of the *American National Standard for Bibliographic References* by the Council of Biology Editors and the American Chemical Society.

80. Llewellyn, Mary E., and Minda M. Sanders. *Citations for nonprint media formats in term papers and theses.* [Lancaster, PA]: Pennsylvania School Librarians Association, 1978. 30p. $2.00 prepaid to the Association at the author's address: 21 North Bausman Drive, Lancaster, PA 17603. [No later editions planned (February 1982).] Bibliography: pp. 27–28.

"Nonprint formats not currently accessible in most school library media centers are excluded from this style manual; i.e., Machine-readable Data File, Videodisc (to date not produced in the United States), etc."

Includes the sequence of description for footnotes and bibliographic citations. The bulk of the manual is devoted to examples of footnotes and bibliographies for the following nonprint materials: chart, diorama, filmstrip, flash card, game, globe, kit, map, microform, microscope slide, model, motion picture, picture, realia, sound recording, transparency, and videorecording. Appendix I contains abbreviations. Appendix II is a glossary for nonprint materials. Indexed.

Bibliographic style: "This manual for nonprint materials follows the format of sample footnote references and corresponding bibliographic entries for print materials in Kate L. Turabian's *A Manual for Writers of Term Papers, Theses, and Dissertations,* 4th ed."

81. McCoy, Florence N. *Researching and writing in history: A practical handbook for students.* Berkeley, CA: University of California Press, [c1974]. xii, 100p. ISBN 0-520-02447-8, ISBN 0-520-02621-7pbk.; LC card 73-76110. $10.95, $4.95pbk. Bibliography: pp. 97–98.

Divided into 12 chapters: 1. introduction, 2–5. collecting the bibliography, 6. reading and note taking: organization is the key, 7. other reference aids: the professional uses them, 8. percolating time: use it to advantage, 9. write: the speaker is yourself, 10. let it cool off: return to this world, 11. edit and rewrite: be your own best enemy, and 12. your paper is done: only clerical details remain. The appendix is entitled "The Student's Home Reference Shelf." A short index is provided.

Bibliographic style: contradictory. The initial citations (pp. 14–16) are not in the style of the final bibliography (pp. 92–93).

"In this handbook I have analyzed the stages involved in the term research paper from the viewpoint of the time involved in each, the order in which they should be undertaken, and their distribution over the typical twelve-week college or university quarter. It is written for the history student, whether graduate or undergraduate, or for any student who faces the task of writing a research paper that involves the use of historical tools and the historical method." This manual is composed of a series of short essays on writing a historical research paper. Because of its poor index and contradictory bibliographical style, the student of history is advised to read McCoy's comments, but to use other style manuals that present the basics of writing and documenting research in an authoritative well-thought-out manner.

82. Manheimer, Martha L. *Style manual: A guide for the preparation of reports and dissertations.* New York: M. Dekker, 1973. vii, 161p. illus. (*Books in library and information science,* 5.) ISBN 0-8247-6046-8; LC card 73-82623. $9.50.

" . . . should be usable for any scholarly paper in the field of library and information science and related areas of study."

"The problem, of course, is that there is often no single correct way of doing anything. The method used should never control the dissertation. This is a particular problem in library and information science because of the wide variety of dissertations possible in this field. They vary from those in which the content seems appropriate for the humanities to others in which the content reflects an orientation towards computer science and related areas. For that reason, probably no fixed format should be prescribed in this field, but the student, in consultation with an advisor, should be permitted to choose the format that seems most appropriate for the subject content of the dissertation."

Bibliographic style: follows *The Chicago Manual of Style.*

Numerous examples of sample pages. Very detailed.

83. Markman, Roberta H., Peter T. Markman, and Marie L. Waddell. *10 steps in writing the research paper.* 3rd ed. Woodbury, NY: Barron's Educational Series, [c1982]. [v], 133 p. ISBN 0-8120-5406-7, ISBN 0-8120-2023-5pbk.; LC card 81-22891. $6.95, $3.95pbk., £2.95, A$5.50, C$4.95. (First ed. 1965; 2nd ed. 1971.)

The 10 steps are: 1. find a subject, 2. read a general article, 3. formulate a temporary thesis and a temporary outline, 4. prepare the preliminary bibliography, 5. take notes from relevant sources, 6. label notecards and revise working outline, 7. write the first draft, 8. revise the text; write introduction and conclusion, 9. fill in footnotes on draft, and 10. put the paper in final form. There are 2 additional sections:

plagiarism: a step to avoid, and the library: a step to master. Appendixes include research terms defined, library classification systems, reference materials and guides, abbreviations, roman numerals, basic punctuation, and footnote and bibliography forms for social and natural sciences. There is a detailed index.

Bibliographic style: identical to that found in *The Chicago Manual of Style*. There are variations from Chicago style, especially in the use of roman numerals discontinued by Turabian and other writers of style manuals. The chapter on bibliography has 45 examples of book and journal titles, including nonprint materials. There are 2 sample bibliographies.

"Arranged to lead the student step by step through the writing of a research paper from finding a suitable subject to checking the final copy. Easy enough for the beginner, complete enough for the graduate student."

The numerous examples of the parts of a research paper are well laid out but lack the highlighting effectively used in the second edition. Also, the table of contents does not record correctly the names of chapters. This is a simplified manual for the college student writing the first research paper.

84. Officer, Lawrence H., Daniel H. Saks, and Judith A. Saks. *So you have to write an economics term paper*. East Lansing, MI: Michigan State University, Graduate School of Business Administration, Division of Research, 1980. x, 149p. ISBN 0-87744-163-4; LC card 80-80313. $2.45pbk. ("The best papers from the M.S.U. economist": pp. [67]–149.) Includes bibliographies.

Part I., how to write an economics term paper, is composed of 12 chapters: 1. a term paper—and it's too late to drop the course: an overview of the problem; 2. what can I tell the prof who knows it all anyway?: the scope for originality, what is a contribution, performing well at your own level, everyone's an expert in something; 3. picking a question that wouldn't strain the resources of the Ford Foundation to answer!: how to find a topic; 4. now that I've got the question how do I get an answer?: choosing a strategy, accident favors the prepared mind, being flexible; 5. you have to open your mouth before you can brush your teeth: breaking down the problem into small sequential tasks with intermediate deadlines; 6. you can't tell it like it is if you don't understand it: analysis, description, opinion, and emotion; 7. facts, true facts, and false facts: types of evidence; 8. finding out what's known even when it's wrong: how to do library research, including books, journals, documents, and newspapers; 9. it's OK to talk to strangers: how to conduct an interview or take a survey; 10. numbers are real and imaginary: how to use statistics; 11. if it's straight from the horse's mouth, you had better name the horse: avoiding plagiarism, preparing footnotes and bibliographies; and 12. getting it together and cutting and pasting: the writing itself, and the importance of editing and revising. Part II. consists of 7 undergraduate papers from the *M.S.U. Economist*. No index is provided.

Bibliographic style: follows Kate L. Turabian's *Student's Guide for Writing College Papers*. Some examples are provided for articles, books, and U.S. government documents.

A concise, well-written manual for undergraduates writing economics term papers. Lively and instructive.

85. Roth, Audrey J. *The research paper: Process, form, and content*. 4th ed. Belmont, CA: Wadsworth Pub. Co. [c1982]. xiii, 242p. ISBN 0-534-01045-8pbk.; LC card 81-11515. $5.95pbk. (First ed. 1966; 2nd ed. 1971; 3rd ed. 1978.) Bibliography: pp. 196–207.

Divided into 9 chapters: 1. starting the research paper, 2. choosing a general topic, 3. narrowing the topic, 4. collecting information, 5. recording information, 6. organizing ideas, 7. writing the paper, 8. documentation, and 9. final presentation. The 4 appendixes are: A. sample research paper, B. selected list of reference works available in libraries, C. bibliography and documentation forms, and D. sample title page. There is a good index.

Bibliographic style: follows the *MLA Handbook for Writers of Research Papers, Theses, and Dissertations*. The extended list of bibliographic citations in appendix C (pp. 208–22) might be missed if only chapter 8 is consulted.

Roth's strategy is to explain as clearly as possible what a research paper is and how a student should move step by step toward the goal of completion. In this 4th edition, Roth has expanded the role of the audience and its importance on the writing process. Examples are extensive throughout the manual, but not excessive. The use of off-red for important sections and chapter headings is very effective. *The Research Paper* is a comprehensive, readable style manual for the college and graduate student. It makes an interesting complement to the *MLA Handbook*.

86. Royal Melbourne Institute of Technology. *Style manual and glossary of terms for use by students of Department of Librarianship, Royal Melbourne Institute of Technology Ltd. in the preparation of papers, essays,* *short reports, etc. and exercises and assignments in cataloguing.* Rev. ed. Editorial supervision: Anton Stavik. [Melbourne]: 1980. 68p.

Divided into 3 parts: part 1. presentation of papers, essays, short papers, etc.; part 2. entries for card catalogue and auxiliary files; and part 3. glossary of terms.

Bibliographic style: author's last name is in capitals, followed by initials (in some cases, first name) with a period. There is then a double en dash with the title in italics. The other elements follow the style presented in the *Anglo-American Cataloguing Rules,* 2nd ed. (Chicago: American Library Association, 1978). Articles in periodicals, books, or government documents use the "in" method. A good description of the elements of bibliography is illustrated with many examples.

Although much of the manual is devoted to sample catalog cards, the initial section on footnotes and bibliography and the glossary of terms at the end are interesting additions to the growth of Australian bibliography.

87. Sayre, John L. *A manual of forms for research papers and D. Min. field project reports.* Enid, OK: Seminary Press, 1981. iv, 46 leaves. ISBN 0-912832-21-5; LC card 81-21521. $4.50. Previously published as: *A manual of forms for term papers and theses.* "D. Min." is Doctor of Ministry.

Divided into 4 parts: 1. format of the research paper, 2. general information on typing the paper, 3. footnotes, and 4. bibliography, with an appendix of sample pages from research papers. Includes index.

Bibliographic style: follows *The Chicago Manual of Style.* In addition to providing bibliographical references for parts of books, multivolumed monographs, periodical articles, encyclopedia articles, newspaper articles, proceedings, scriptural and classifical references, theses, dissertations, manuscripts, letters, interviews, minutes, and class lecture notes, there are numerous examples specifically for the Bible and other religious works.

"For points not covered in this guide, and for more illustrations, students should consult Kate L. Turabian's *A Manual for Writers of Term Papers, Theses and Dissertations,* 4th ed.; University of Chicago's *Manual of Style,* 12th ed.; John Taylor's *Manual of Bibliographical and Footnote Forms;* and his *Illustrated Guide to Abbreviations for Use in Religious Studies.*" This manual is useful as one of the religious extensions of Chicago style.

88. Seeber, Edward D. *A style manual for students: For the preparation of term papers, essays, and theses.* 3rd ed., rev. Bloomington, IN: Indiana University Press, [1976, c1967]. 94p. ([*A Midland book,* MB 67.]) ISBN 0-253-20067-9; LC card 67-11623; OCLC 409 0142. Out of print. (Issued earlier in 1964, 1967, and 1968.)

Corresponds "generally to the *Style Sheet* of the Modern Language Association . . . This guide for authors of term papers, scholarly reports, theses and dissertations explains in simple and understandable terms, and illustrates with copious examples and specimen pages, the accepted principles of typescript preparation, the use of quoted matter, the correct forms of footnotes and bibliography, and the makeup of parts such as title page, table of contents, and index. The manual deals liberally with punctuation, capitalization, foreign-language problems (titles of published works, proper names, word division, etc.), and other matters indispensable for the achievement of correctness, clarity, readability, consistency, and good appearance."

Bibliographic style: follows the Modern Language Association *Style Sheet* with its roman numerals for volume numbers of periodicals. Provided are 6 pages of bibliographic entries.

Pragmatic treatment, but excessive use of ellipses for parts of titles. A succinct manual, good for its numerous examples, but instructions are too brief to permit extensive coverage of any given topic. Good index. Updated by *MLA Handbook* (*see* item 165).

89. Smith, Charles B. *A guide to business research: Developing, conducting, and writing research projects.* Chicago: Nelson-Hall, [c1981]. viii, 190p. ISBN 0-88229-546-2text, ISBN 0-88229-730-3pbk.; LC card 79-22991. $18.95 text ed., $8.95pbk. Bibliography: pp. 181–85.

Divided into 9 chapters: 1. characterizing research, 2. selecting and developing the research problem, 3. designing the research strategy, 4. searching documentary sources, 5. collecting survey data, 6. developing the outline, 7. writing the introduction, 8. writing the content chapters, and 9. writing the terminal chapter. The 4 appendixes are: A. collecting data from documentary sources, B. constructing a title page, C. writing an abstract for the research report, and D. evaluating the research report. Lists of "Suggested Reading" conclude some chapters.

Bibliographic style: no bibliographic style is presented; however, the author follows *The Chicago Manual of Style* in his own bibliography and suggested reading lists.

"The purpose of this book is to help business students with their research projects, theses, or dissertations. . . .

"The book is intended for undergraduate and graduate research and report writing. . . ." Smith presents a step-by-step approach to writing papers. In particular, he focuses on the formation of the hypothesis statement and the collection of data from documentary sources. This guide is up to date, concise, and well presented.

90. Sternberg, Robert J. *Writing the psychology paper.* Woodbury, NY: Barron's Educational Series, [c1977]. x, 243, 6p. ISBN 0-8120-0772-7; LC card 77-9250. $3.95.

Divided into 9 parts: 1. eight common misconceptions about psychology papers, 2. steps in writing the library research paper, 3. steps in writing the experimental research paper, 4. rules for writing the psychology paper, 5. commonly misused words, 6. American Psychological Association guidelines for psychology papers (summarizing the grammar and reference parts of the *Publication Manual of the American Psychological Association*, 2nd ed.), 7. references for the psychology paper (names and addresses of 74 reference works and journals), 8. standards for evaluating the psychology paper, and 9. submitting a paper to a journal. The appendix is a sample paper typed according to APA guidelines. Indexed.

Bibliographic style: follows the *Publications Manual of the American Psychological Association.* Only a few examples of bibliographic style are presented.

Sternberg's position on the style of the Modern Language Association of America is pertinent to understanding his manual: "A common mistake occurs when students follow Modern Language Association guidelines, which are the ones most students learn in high school. Although these guidelines are appropriate for writing in the humanities, they are not appropriate for writing in psychology." This guide is for undergraduate and graduate students. Relatively few examples are used in the text, which is prescriptive in nature.

91. *A style manual for college students: A guide to written assignments and research papers,* [by Margaret L. Ranald, et al.]. [Flushing, NY?]: Queens College Press, [c1976]. 41p. ISBN 0-930146-07-7. $1.00.

"This style manual was originally prepared for the guidance of undergraduate students at Queens College of the City University of New York." Divided into 8 parts: writing standards and procedures, preparation of papers, manuscript format, plagiarism and how to avoid it, documentation, quotation techniques, footnotes, and bibliography. Indexed.

Bibliographic style: for books, it follows *The Chicago Manual of Style.* For periodical articles, the style is unique. Gives examples for books, translations, series, edited books, articles, essays, chapters, speeches, short poems, encyclopedia articles, pamphlets, and government documents.

A good elementary manual.

92. Teitelbaum, Harry. *How to write theses: A guide to the research paper.* [New York]: Monarch Press, [1975, c1966]. [vii], 136p. ISBN 0-671-18726-0. $1.95.

Divided into 12 chapters: 1. so you have a research paper to write, 2. the library, 3. the working bibliography, 4. note-taking, 5. writing the paper, 6. the format of the research paper, 7. quotations, 8. footnote references, 9. the bibliography, 10. tables, graphs, illustrations, 11. the final manuscript, and 12. the shorter theme. The 3 appendixes are: 1. sample notecards and research paper, 2. additional footnote and bibliography forms, and 3. abbreviations and symbols used in footnotes and bibliographies. No index is provided.

Bibliographic style: follows *The Chicago Manual of Style.*

A detailed manual that pays serious attention to construction of a thesis step by step. Unfortunately, the lack of an index prevents its use as a reference aid during writing.

93. Turabian, Kate L. *A manual for writers of research papers, theses, and dissertations.* British ed. prepared by John E. Spink. London: Heinemann, 1982. 227p. illus. ISBN 0-434-79970-Xpbk.; £3.95.

Divided into 13 parts: 1. the parts of a paper, 2. abbreviations, contractions and numbers, 3. spelling and punctuation, 4. capitalization, underlining and other matters of style, 5. quotations, 6. footnotes, 7. bibliographies, 8. sample footnote references and corresponding bibliographical entries, 9. official publications, 10. tables, 11. illustrations, 12. scientific papers, and 13. typing the paper. The 3 appendixes are: 1. compiling an index, 2. correcting proofs, and 3. useful British standards. Indexed.

"The *Manual* is primarily directed at those who are preparing academic work to meet the requirements of institutions of higher learning, or who are presenting papers for publication in scholarly periodicals.

It is hoped, however, that it will also provide guidance for those who are undertaking work at the secondary and further levels of education.''

Bibliographic style: Spink makes few changes from Turabian's American version (*see* item 94): ''I have occasionally rearranged paragraphs to bring British material into greater prominence and I have made alterations of detail to comply with British styles of citation. Only the section on the treatment of legal documents has required substantial revision. I have retained most of the American examples as to change them would seem pedantic, especially since the American contribution to most fields of research is significant.''

94. Turabian, Kate L. *A manual for writers of term papers, theses, and dissertations*. 4th ed. Chicago: University of Chicago Press, [1973]. viii, 216p. ISBN 0-226-81620-6, ISBN 0-226-81621-4pbk.; LC card 73-77792. $12.00, $3.95pbk. [First edition (1937) and 2nd edition (1955) have title: *A manual for writers of dissertations;* 3rd ed. 1967.]

Divided into 13 chapters: 1. the parts of the paper, 2. abbreviations and numbers, 3. spelling and punctuation, 4. capitalization, underlining, and other matters, 5. quotations, 6. footnotes, 7. bibliographies, 8. sample footnote references and corresponding bibliographical entries, 9. public documents, 10. tables, 11. illustrations, 12. scientific papers, and 13. typing the paper. A good index is provided.

Bibliographic style: Turabian's manual is based on the principles and guidelines found in *The Chicago Manual of Style* (12th ed.). However, Turabian's manual contains many more examples, making it a ready companion for the student working on a paper or thesis.

Instead of placing the emphasis on publication, *A Manual for Writers of Term Papers, Theses, and Dissertations* is designed for typewritten presentation of formal papers in the scientific and nonscientific fields. The preface includes a brief history of the manual's development. Certain Latin abbreviations in footnotes have been removed from this edition, and the section on punctuation has been expanded.

Turabian has compiled a detailed manual rich in examples that aim to provide answers to individual questions. This manual presents a more sophisticated approach to problems of style than is found in her *Student's Guide for Writing College Papers* (*see* item 95). Additional aid may be found by consulting *The Chicago Manual of Style*.

95. Turabian, Kate L. *Student's guide for writing college papers*. 3rd ed. Chicago: University of Chicago Press, [1976]. viii, 256p. ISBN 0-226-

81622-2, 0-226-81623-0pbk.; LC card 76-435. $12.00, $4.50pbk. Bibliography: p. 183–244. (First ed. 1963; 2nd ed. 1969.)

Divided into 7 chapters: 1. introduction, 2. choosing a topic, 3. collecting material, 4. planning the paper, 5. writing the paper, 6. some matters of style, and 7. footnote and bibliographic forms. Appendix A is a sample research paper, and Appendix B is a select list of reference works chosen by Donald F. Bond, Professor Emeritus of English, University of Chicago.

Bibliographic style: follows and elaborates upon the style found in *The Chicago Manual of Style*.

" . . . designed for high school, junior college, or college students faced with writing their first long documented paper." Step-by-step approach with more considered explanation of the elements of a paper than in Turabian's *A Manual for Writers of Term Papers, Theses, and Dissertations* (*see* item 94). Good, detailed instructions on how to use a research library are illustrated with many examples clarifying the construction of bibliographies and footnotes. Some sections, namely those on footnotes, punctuation, numbers, and spelling, overlap with similar material in *A Manual for Writers of Term Papers, Theses, and Dissertations*. The list of reference works (pp. 183–244) is long, detailed, and unique to this guide.

96. Winkler, Anthony C., and Jo Ray McCuen. *Writing the research paper: A handbook*. New York: Harcourt Brace Jovanovich, [c1979]. xii, 276p. ISBN 0-15-598290-7; LC card 78-73967. $6.95.

Divided into 13 chapters: 1. basic information about the research paper, 2. choosing a topic, 3. the library, 4. finding background sources, 5. doing the research, 6. the thesis and the outline, 7. transforming the notes into a rough draft, 8. punctuation, mechanics, and spelling, 9. documentation, 10. bibliography, 11. preparing the final typescript, 12. a sample student paper, and 13. a brief guide to writing about literature. Indexed.

Bibliographic style: follows the *MLA Handbook for Writers of Research Papers, Theses, and Dissertations*.

"*Writing the Research Paper: A Handbook* unabashedly resembles a dictionary. No one part of this book is dependent for the continuity upon another. Instead, the process of writing a research paper is atomized and presented in minuscule steps that are carefully explained and catalogued under separate, indexed heads." Its unorthodox arrangement makes this handbook somewhat more difficult to use than other style manuals.

97. Yaggy, Elinor. *How to write your term paper.* 4th ed. New York: Harper & Row, [c1980]. xi, 84p. ISBN 0-06-047295-2; LC card 79-18032. $5.50. (First ed. 1959; 3rd ed. 1974.)

> Divided into 8 chapters: I. preview of this book, II. your audience, III. choosing and narrowing your topic, IV. assembling your material, V. organizing your material, VI. writing the paper, VII. assembling the finished paper, and VIII. a sample term paper. Appendix A contains variant forms for footnotes and bibliographic items. Appendix B has abbreviations, and Appendix C includes a chart of roman numerals and an explanation of their use.

> Bibliographic style: "follows the second edition of the *MLA Style Sheet* and the *MLA Handbook.*"

> A concise manual with many illustrative examples. Thorough discussions of difficult areas, e.g., conflicting sources. A good supplement to the *MLA Handbook for Writers of Research Papers, Theses, and Dissertations.* The copy examined was printed on poor-quality paper.

UNIVERSITY PRESSES

98. Brigham Young University Press. *Author, publisher: The happy combination.* [Provo, UT: 1976.] 15p.

> Divided into 4 major parts: the role of the press including the particular fields of interest, submitting your manuscript, acceptance of your manuscript, and publication of your book.

> Bibliographic style: follows *The Chicago Manual of Style.*

99. *Cambridge authors' and printers' guides.* Nos. 1–7. Cambridge [Eng.]: Cambridge University Press, 1951–69. (Superseded in part by *Cambridge authors' and publishers' guides.*) (*see* item 100.)

> [no.] 1. Morison, Stanley. *First principles of typography.* 2nd ed. 1967. 24p. LC card 67-26070. Out of print. (First published 1930.) (First edition 1951 in this series.)

> [no.] 2. Crutchley, Brooke. *Preparation of manuscripts and correction of proofs.* 6th ed. 1970. 19p. illus. ISBN 0-521-07864-4; LC card 79-112467. $3.95. (First ed. 1951; 2nd ed. 1964; 3rd ed. 1965; 4th ed. 1967; 5th ed. 1968.)

> Includes sections on the manuscript, printed copy, make-up of books, letterpress and lithography, illustrations, notes, quotations, headings,

page heads, cross-references, tables and pedigrees, bibliography and references, index, special signs, style, and correcting proof.

[no.] 3. Carey, Gordon V. *Making an index.* 2nd ed. 1951. 15p. LC card A53-2832. Out of print. (First ed. 1951.)

Includes index.

[no.] 4. Burbidge, Peter G. *Notes and references.* 1952. 19p. ISBN 0-521-07518-1; LC card A54-296. $1.75.

Includes a discussion of footnotes, endnotes, sidenotes, and lists of references.

[no.] 5. Ewart, Kenneth. *Copyright.* 1952. 18p. Out of print.

Out of date.

[no.] 6. Carey, Gordon V. *Punctuation.* Appendix by P. G. Burbidge. 1957. vi, 40p. LC card A58-3931. Out of print.

[no.] 7. Burbidge, Peter G. *Prelims and end-pages.* 2nd ed. 1969. 31p. ISBN 0-521-07508-4; LC card 77-518846. $3.95. (First ed. 1963.)

The prelims consist of the order of the make-up: the half-title; the verso of the half-title; the title-page; the verso of the title-page; the dedication; the contents and list of illustrations; and the preface, foreword, and introduction. The end pages consist of the appendixes, notes, bibliography, the index, and the colophon.

100. *Cambridge authors' and publishers' guides.* Cambridge [Eng.]: Cambridge University Press, 1971–. (Supersedes in part *Cambridge authors' and printers' guides.)*

The following unnumbered titles have been identified:

Anderson, Margaret Dampier (Whetham). *Book indexing.* 1979. iv, 36p. ISBN 0-521-08202-1; LC card 70-154517. $3.95. (First published 1971.)

Includes index. Pragmatic approach to making an index.

Butcher, Judith. *Typescripts, proofs and indexes.* 1980. 32 p. ISBN 0-521-29739-7; LC card 79-52666. $2.95.

Includes sections on illustrations, spelling and other conventions, cross-references, headings, headlines or running heads, tables, quotations, copyright permissions, footnotes and endnotes, bibliographical references, science and mathematics, correcting proofs, and making an index.

Scarles, Christopher. *Copyright.* 1980. 32p. ISBN 0-521-29740-0; LC card 18401. $3.50.

Includes information on copyright in the United Kingdom and the United States.

Trevitt, John. *Book design.* 1980. iv, 34p. ISBN 0-521-29741-9; LC card 79-20194. $3.50.

Includes sections on printing processes, choice of page size, typesetting, typefaces, margins, justified and unjustified setting, centered and asymmetrical layouts, subheadings, pageheads, headings, tables, quotations, footnotes, endnotes, bibliographies, indexes, preliminary pages, illustrations, paper, binding, and jackets and covers.

101. Clarendon Press. *Notes on the preparation of manuscripts for publication.* [Oxford]: University Press, [197–]. 13p.

Includes brief information on "Copy, Copy Order, Punctuation, Abbreviations, Capitals, Italics, Spelling, Honours and Titles, Time Phrases, Dating, Figures, Sections and Subsections, Bibliography, List of Sources, etc., Footnotes, Illustrations, Figures and Maps, Correction in Proof, Index, Marking up Copy, [and] A Few Reference Books." There follow 3 unnumbered pages of "Symbols for Correcting Proof."

Bibliographic style: last name may be in capitals with titles of books and journals in italics. Parentheses enclose publisher, place of publication and date, in that order. Titles of journal articles and unpublished books and articles are placed in single quotes, called "inverted commas" by Clarendon. Other usages such as omitting "vol." and "p." are unique and should be studied before using the Clarendon system.

102. Cornell University Press. *The preparation of manuscript and illustrations.* [Ithaca, NY: 197–.] 8 unnumbered pages.

"House styling at Cornell University Press is adaptable to an author's needs and wishes." The pamphlet includes short sections on quotations, illustrations, and other style manuals (*The MLA Style Sheet, The Chicago Manual of Style,* and *Words into Type*). More attention is given to footnotes and bibliography.

Bibliographic style: for books, Cornell follows *The Chicago Manual of Style.* For articles in periodicals, some variation is permitted with 3 styles represented: one with, another without abbreviations, and the third, the Harvard format.

103. Indiana University Press. [*Author's manual.*] Bloomington, IN: [197–?]. 8p.

Divided into 14 parts: typing the manuscript; reprinted material; styling; checking; revise the manuscript, not the proof; production schedules must be kept; steps in producing a book; notes and footnotes; permissions; illustrations; mailing proof and manuscripts; change of address; sales and promotion; and author's copies. "Indiana University press editors follow the guidelines set forth in the CHICAGO MANUAL OF STYLE. We index according to the booklet by Sina Spiker, INDEXING YOUR BOOK: A PRACTICAL GUIDE FOR AUTHORS, or by the Chicago guidelines."

Bibliographic style: no bibliographic style is presented. Presumably follows *The Chicago Manual of Style*.

104. Iowa State University Press. *Memorandum for authors: A guidebook.* Ames, IA: [1979]. Pamphlet (24p.)

Divided into 11 parts: introduction, notes on manuscript preparation, editorial processing of manuscript, indexing, multiauthor works, manuscript preparation for a revised edition, promotion, authors' copies, copyright protection, acknowledgments and permissions, and sample permission letter. "We use the University of Chicago Press *A Manual of Style* for solving most of our editorial problems and have no formal press style sheet of our own."

Bibliographic style: "The Iowa State University Press recommends the Chicago *Manual of Style* (which takes account of these special differences among disciplines), or the preferred style manual in your field."

105. The Johns Hopkins University Press. *From manuscript to bound book.* Baltimore, MD: [c1978]. Pamphlet (12 unnumbered p.)

Divided into 4 parts: preparing the manuscript for editing and production, copyediting the manuscript, producing the book, and marketing the book.

Bibliographic style: no bibliographic style is presented. However, the press follows *The Chicago Manual of Style*.

105a. Lagos University Press. *Guide to authors.* [Lagos, Nigeria]: 1981. 15p.

Divided into 2 parts of numbered sections: part 1, preparation of typescript includes the following sections: 1. notes/footnotes, 2. bibliography and references (general), 3. references and bibliography: natural science and social sciences, 4. changes and revisions, 5. permissions, 6. quoted matter, 7. tables, 8. figures/illustrations, 9. [not used], 10. to the general editor of a collection of papers or an anthology, 11. preliminary pages, and 12. style. Part 2, the edited script, includes the following sections: 1. author's check-of-editing, 2. schedules, 3. proofreading, 4. alterations, and compiling the index. Proofreader's marks and a work schedule on manuscripts accepted for publication complete this guide.

Bibliographic style: ''For a book, the full citation should include: author's (editor's) name in full; title in full (in italics); place of publication; name of publisher (for twentieth century books); date of publication; volume number, page number or the like.

''For an article, the full citation should include: author's name in full; title of the article (in quotation marks); title of the periodical (in italics); volume number, issue number and/or date, and page reference.

''Lagos University Press took off as a printing and publishing concern in 1981. Before then, printing activities of the University were carried out on a small scale in the Library.''

Examples of style would enhance the value of this first author's guide from Africa.

106. Oxford University Press. *Hart's rules for compositors and readers at the University Press, Oxford.* 38th ed., completely rev. Oxford: [c1978]. xii, 184p. ISBN 0-19-212969-4; £4.95. Bibliography: p. 135. New edition in preparation.

''Originally compiled by Horace Hart, M.A., Printer to the University, 1883–1915. First edition, 1893. Fifteenth edition (the first for general sale), 1904. Thirty-seventh edition, 1967.''

Hart's rules are prescriptive and deeply rooted in the printer's experience. The manual is divided into 3 parts: rules for setting English, spellings, and rules for setting foreign languages. Rules for setting English includes sections on biological nomenclature, capitals, figures and numerals, italic and roman type, punctuation, quotations, scientific work, etc. Spellings includes sections on the formation of plurals in words of foreign origin, words ending in ''-able,'' etc. Rules for setting foreign languages includes sections on French, German, Greek and Latin, Italian, oriental languages in roman type, Russian, Spanish, Catalan and Portuguese, and Turkish. The appendix, rules for composition and make-up, includes sections on the division of words, footnotes, illustrations, new chapters or sections, plays, poetry, spacing, tables, and sample figures. A detailed index is provided.

Bibliographic style: no bibliographic style is presented, but a footnote style is provided.

This oldest of all contemporary style manuals concentrates on punctuation, spelling, and the typography of foreign languages. A companion volume to *Hart's Rules* is *The Oxford Dictionary for Writers and Editors* (Oxford: Clarendon Press, 1981. xiv, 448p.), in which " 'Writers and editors' are the main concern of the dictionary, and it therefore no longer caters directly or extensively for the needs of printers except in so far as those needs are shared by writers and editors in their dealings with publishers and printers." The 2 titles, *Hart's Rules* and *The Oxford Dictionary for Writers and Editors* together create a complete presentation of the house style of Oxford University Press. For a contrasting presentation of rules for foreign languages, see the *Style Manual* (item 52) published by the Government Printing Office of the United States.

107. Pennsylvania State University Press. *Guidelines for preparation of book manuscripts.* [University Park, PA: 1979.] 6 leaves.

Divided into 10 parts: manuscripts required by the press, preparing the manuscript, matters of style, a note on notes, camera-ready text copy, illustrations, permissions, alterations in proof, the preface, and miscellaneous.

"When in doubt consult standard authorities such as the Chicago *Manual of Style. . . ."*

Bibliographic style: no bibliographic style is presented.

108. Princeton University Press. *Memorandum for authors, editors, compositors [and] proofreaders on the preparation of manuscripts and the handling of proof.* [Princeton, NJ?: 197–.] 24p.

An in-house manual with brief discussions of punctuation, spelling, dates, numbers, quotations, abbreviations, and italics. A separate section covers the preparation of the manuscript including notes, cross-references, bibliography, illustrations, science manuscripts, and copyrighted material. The final section, handling proof, includes information on galley proofs, running heads, page proof, marking proof, author's alterations, and the index.

Bibliographic style: no bibliographic style is presented. However, for footnote style the writer is referred to the *MLA Style Sheet,* 2nd ed., and *The Chicago Manual of Style.*

109. Ryan, Peter A. *The preparation of manuscripts.* [Carlton, Victoria]: Melbourne University Press, [1966, reprinted 1975]. 23p. ISBN 0-522-83728-X; LC card 67-99863. A$.60. (Distributed in the United States by International Scholarly Book Service for $3.00.)

"The idea for this pamphlet arose from a discussion on scholarly publishing held in 1962, between members of the Australian Humanities Research Council and the Australian Book Publishers' Association." It is divided into 11 sections: editor and typesetter, typewriter and typist, consistency, footnotes, headings, tables, illustrations, assembling your manuscript, proofs, copyright, and conclusion.

Bibliographic style: no bibliographic style is presented.

110. Southern Illinois University Press. *Manuscript preparation.* [Carbondale, IL: 197–.] 12 leaves.

Covers the order of the manuscript, holdings and subheadings, extracts, notes, bibliographies and reference lists, glossaries and lists of abbreviations, tables, charts, figures and maps, legends for illustrations, indexes, insertions, the use of ellipses, transliteration, mathematical signs and symbols, permissions, illustrations, and a brief check list.

Bibliographic style: "For other matters of style we generally follow *A Manual of Style,* Twelfth Edition (Chicago: University of Chicago Press, 1969), which enjoys international acceptance by both scholarly and commercial publishers. . . ."

111. Sydney University Press. *A guide to authors in the preparation of manuscripts.* [Sydney: 197–.] 11p.

Divided into 3 parts. The first, press style and the preparation of manuscripts, covers preliminary pages, headings, italics, spelling, hyphenation, abbreviations and contractions, countries and organizations, figures, quotations, square brackets, paragraphs, footnotes, tabular matter, bibliography, index, and illustrations. The second section covers the typing of the manuscript, and the third includes material on reading and correcting proofs.

Bibliographic style: no bibliographic style is presented. Footnote style is not unlike that published in *The Chicago Manual of Style,* but is differently punctuated. Few abbreviations are used.

112. University of Alabama Press. *Guidelines for authors.* [University, AL: 197–.] Pamphlet (6p.) fold.

Divided into 7 sections: the anatomy of a book, concerning copyright, preparation of the manuscript, manners of style, from manuscript to book, on writing, and author's checklist.

Bibliographic style: "In notes and in bibliographical entries, the place of publication, the complete name of the publisher, and the date of publication should be given, in that order. . . . The Press prefers a full bibliography." Otherwise, *The Chicago Manual of Style* is used for notes and bibliographies.

113. University of Chicago Press. *The Chicago manual of style.* 13th ed., rev. and expanded. Chicago: [1982]. ix, 737p., illus. ISBN 0-226-10390-0; LC card 82-2832. $25.00. ("For authors, editors, and copywriters.") (First–12th editions have title: *A Manual of style for authors, editors and copywriters;* First ed. 1906; 2nd ed. 1910; 3rd ed. 1911; 4th ed. 1914; 5th ed. 1917; 6th ed. 1919; 7th ed. 1920; 8th ed. 1925; 9th ed. 1927; 10th ed. 1937; 11th ed. 1949; 12th ed. 1969. These earlier editions are cataloged by most libraries under: Chicago. University. Press.) Bibliography: pp. 685–94.

The current edition of *The Chicago Manual of Style* is divided into 3 parts: bookmaking, style, and production and printing. The first part covers chapters on 1. the parts of a book, 2. manuscript preparation and copyediting, 3. proofs, and 4. rights and permissions. Part 2 includes chapters on 5. punctuation, 6. spelling and distinctive treatment of words, 7. names and terms, 8. numbers, 9. foreign languages in type, 10. quotations, 11. illustrations, captions, and legends, 12. tables, 13. mathematics in type, 14. abbreviations, 15. documentation: references, notes, and bibliographies, 16. bibliographic forms, 17. note forms, and 18. indexes. Part 3 includes chapters on 19. design and typography and 20. composition, printing, and binding. A glossary of technical terms is followed by an annotated and evaluative bibliography of style manuals, general dictionaries, aids in indexing, writer's guides, and other reference books. The index is good, but some knowledge of the layout of the manual and its tables of contents is needed to use the book effectively.

Bibliographic style: chapters 15–17 on bibliographic style have been greatly expanded with this edition. Two basic styles are presented: Chicago style called type "A," and author-date style (elsewhere known as "scientific style" or "Harvard style") called type "B." They are discussed concurrently, a departure from earlier editions of the manual. Other types of bibliographic styles, such as that represented in the *American National Standard for Bibliographic References* used in the fields of biology, chemistry, and the medical sciences, are ignored. The addition of tables of examples to this edition increases the usefulness of the manual.

The Chicago manual is the most widely used style manual in North America. Its chief advantage lies in its exhaustive treatment of the publishing process with copious examples used throughout the text. For the Chicago style in the United Kingdom, *see* Turabian (item 93). Additional help is provided in a useful section entitled "For Further Reference," at the end of each chapter where supplemental titles are cited. This expanded edition of the Chicago manual is recommended for anyone wishing to publish in North America.

114. University of Michigan Press. *Author's guide: Manuscript preparation and the production process*. Ann Arbor, MI: [197–?]. 17p.

Divided into 2 parts. Part one, preparation of manuscript, includes information on chapter titles and subheads, quotations, notes or footnotes, figure legends (titles), tables, glossaries and lists of abbreviations, bibliographies and reference lists, indexes, permissions, duration of copyright, letters and diaries, published journal articles, checking and correcting the manuscript, numbering pages, illustrative material, manuscript preparation from printed materials and for collected works, and transmission of the manuscript. Part two, the production process, covers manuscript editing, production scheduling, proofs and indexing, and proofreader's marks.

Bibliographic style: "Type authors' names in an alphabetical list, last name first, double space. If several works by the same author are listed, type a dash (three or four typed hyphens) with period in place of the author's name."

"The Press recommends the latest edition of *A Manual of Style*, The University of Chicago Press, in the preparation of your manuscript."

115. University of Missouri Press. *Author's information*. [Columbia, MO: 197–.] Pamphlet (11p.)

Includes 10 topics: revisions, house editing, titling, design, permissions, production, promotion, publication date, author's copies, and royalty payments.

Bibliographic style: follows *The Chicago Manual of Style*. The press also issues instructions on *Manuscript Submission* (4p.).

116. University of Oklahoma Press. [*Author's guide.*] Norman, OK: [between 197– and 1981]. 5p. (1 sheet fold. to 6.)

Divided into 7 sections: dictionaries and manuals, manuscript form, professional jargon, illustrations and maps, proofs, time factors, and publicity.

Bibliographic style: "Bibliographies may be handled alphabetically, classified, or as presented in Pritchard's *Criticism in America*. If appended as alphabetical or classified affairs, they should be arranged as hanging indentions and double-spaced. . . ."

For style, including bibliographic style, the University of Oklahoma Press uses *The Chicago Manual of Style*. Oklahoma also has a similar publication entitled: *About Making Your Index* ([4p.]).

117. University of South Carolina Press. *Guidelines for authors.* [Columbia, SC]: 1979. Pamphlet (12p.)

Divided into 5 parts: copyright, looking for a publisher, preparing your manuscript, proofreading, and indexes.

Bibliographic style: *The Chicago Manual of Style.*

"If you want formulas for punctuation, footnotes, bibliographical citations, and the like, we recommend the famous *Manual of Style* published by the University of Chicago Press."

118. University of Tennessee Press. *A guide for authors.* [Knoxville, TN: 197–.] 9p.

"This booklet has been prepared with the 'first-book author' in mind, but we hope as well that more experienced authors will find it useful."

"We make no attempt to impose our taste and style on the author in the text portion of a MS, except to request the use of first preference American spellings. Therefore we do not have a mandatory house style for capitalization or other minor points; in short, as long as an author is consistent in his usage and employs acceptable standards of grammar, punctuation, and the like, we allow the author his hand."

Bibliographic style: "If a bibliography or bibliographical essay is supplied (which we invariably recommend), only an author's last name and a short title need appear in the first footnote reference. We will, however, honor the request to include complete publication data in the first footnote reference."

The University of Tennessee Press also issues: *Important Instructions to Authors* (2 leaves); *A Note for Authors on Preparing the Index* (2p.); and *A Note for Authors on Preparing Copy for Editing* (2p.).

119. University of Texas Press. *A guide for authors*. Austin, TX; London: [c1978]. 28p.

Divided into 3 parts. Part 1, preparing your book for publication, includes the typed copy, tables, illustrations, permissions, documentation, and general style. Part 2, the publication process, includes steps toward publication, indexes, multiauthored works, and camera-ready copy. Part 3, other information, includes marketing, journals, rights and permissions, royalties, and author's discount.

Bibliographic style: "For a more thorough discussion of notes, bibliographies, and citations in general, see the twelfth revised edition (1969) of *A Manual of Style*, published by the University of Chicago Press, pp. 337–397. We follow this manual in most instances."

120. University of Washington Press. *The preparation of manuscripts: A memorandum for authors*. Seattle, WA: [1976]. 17p. (First ed. 1967; rev. ed. 1970.)

Divided into 15 sections: preparation of the manuscript, illustrations, spelling, quotations, permissions, subheads, enumerations, capitalization, italics, numbers, dates, possessives, miscellaneous rules of punctuation, notes, and bibliography.

Bibliographic style: follows *The Chicago Manual of Style*.

121. University of Western Australia Press. *Instruction to authors on style and preparation of manuscripts*. [Nedlands: 197–.] 10p.

Divided into 13 major sections: manuscripts, subdivisions, style, dictionary, italics and roman, numerals, quotations, text figures, plates, tables, galley proofs, page proofs, and referencing system for nonscientific works.

Bibliographic style: follows John Pitson's *Style Manual of Authors, Editors and Printers of Australian Government Publications*. The press also issues *The Harvard System for Scientific Works* (5p.).

122. University Press of Northern [deleted] New England. *The preparation of manuscript and illustrations*. Hanover, NH: 1970. Pamphlet (10p.)

Includes sections on consistency of style, quoted material, the author's notes, the bibliography, permission to use copyrighted material, and the preparation of illustrations.

Bibliographic style: "For books a standard form is as follows: (1) author's name (last name first), followed by a period; (2) title of the book (usually underscored to indicate italics), followed by a period; (3) number and description of edition (3d ed., rev. and enl.) if needed, followed by a period; (4) number of volumes (3 vols.) if more than one; (5) place of publication, followed by a colon; (6) name of the publisher (sometimes omitted), followed by a comma; and (7) year of publication, followed by a period."

"Periodical references in scientific journals vary greatly in style. It is suggested that the author consult the leading journal in his field and follow its form."

The University Press of New England also has a pamphlet entitled *Reading Proof and Preparing an Index* (8p.).

123. University Press of Virginia. *The preparation of manuscript and illustrations.* [Charlottesville, VA: 1964, rev. 1979.] [11]p.

Divided into 2 parts. Part one is called preparation of manuscript and includes consistency of style, quoted material, the author's notes, the bibliography, permission to use copyrighted material, and typing a camera-ready manuscript. The second part is on the preparation of illustrations.

Bibliographic style: "Bibliographical forms differ markedly, and unfortunately, no one form can be recommended for use with all types of material." The citations to books follow *The Chicago Manual of Style*. The citations to periodical articles show 2 different styles: one unique and the other, Harvard style.

124. University Presses of Florida. *Authors' guide.* [Gainesville?, FL: 197–.] 10 leaves.

Divided into 2 major parts: (1) preparation of the manuscript, including contents of the manuscript and sending the manuscript, and (2) styling the contents of the manuscript, including sections on the text, chapter titles and subheads, front and back matter, bibliography, notes, tables, illustrations, and quoted material and poetry.

Bibliographic style: *The Chicago Manual of Style*. Alternative style: Harvard as presented in *The Chicago Manual of Style*.

Subject Manuals*

AGRICULTURE

General Style

125. American Society of Agronomy. *Handbook and style manual for ASA, CSSA, and SSSA publications.* [6th ed.] Madison, WI: American Society of Agronomy; Crop Science Society of America; Soil Science Society of America, 1976. v, 97p. illus. ISBN 0-891-18042-7. $3.00. [First edition (1948) has title: *Notes to contributors;* 4th ed. 1967; 5th ed. 1971.] Bibliography: pp. 93–94.

> Divided into 9 chapters: 1. introduction, 2. publications of the societies, 3. descriptions and procedures for society journals, 4. descriptions and procedures for other society publications, 5. details of style, 6. preparing the manuscript, 7. proofreading, 8. responsibilities for review and publication management, and 9. guide for preparation of monographs. Appendix A includes a sample letter to obtain permission to use copyrighted material. Appendix B is a list of abbreviations for journal titles. Indexed.

> ''This handbook and style manual will serve as a guide for writing, reviewing, and editing papers submitted to all publications of the societies. It is based on several sources, especially the *CBE Style Manual* [3rd ed., 1972] published by the American Institute of Biological Sciences for the Council of Biology Editors.''

> Bibliographic style: Harvard. Examples are given for transactions, bulletins, agronomy monograph series, technical or other reports, foreign-language periodicals, advances in agronomy, chapters in books, journal articles, patents, dissertations, books, miscellaneous publications, society publications, U.S. state publications, and U.S.

---

*The following subject manuals (items 125–226) are divided, where relevant, into 2 sections: ''general style'' and ''journal style.'' The directories of journal style omit reference to any one bibliographic style; therefore, this element is not included in the discussion.

government publications. For additional examples, the writer is referred to the *CBE Style Manual*. Periodical titles are abbreviated from the *Bibliographic Guide for Editors and Authors* (Washington, DC: American Chemical Society, 1974). In addition to the style for the societies' publications—*Agronomy Journal* (ASA), *Journal of Agronomic Education* (ASA), *Journal of Environmental Quality* (ASA, CSSA, and SSSA), *Crop Science* (CSSA), and *Soil Science Society of America Journal* (SSSA)—a discussion of style in regard to the following details is provided: elemental expression for plant nutrients; reports of crop yields; nomenclature; numerals; measurements, metric system; statistics; spelling and capitalization; punctuation; and abbreviations and symbols.

This is the only up-to-date style manual specifically for agriculture and agricultural research.

126. Australia. Standing Committee on Agriculture. *Guidelines for the preparation of manuscripts*. Canberra: [Printed by CSIRO, Melbourne], 1979. 7p. *(Standing Committee on Agriculture technical report series.)* ISBN 0-643-00340-1.

Guidelines for the publication of reports and papers prepared by expert panels, working parties for the Standing Committee on Agriculture. These notes apply only to the ''SCA Technical Reports,'' which are to be published in part by the Commonwealth Scientific and Industrial Research Organization in an effort to make the reports more accessible to interested parties.

Bibliographic style: Harvard.

AREA STUDIES

Journal Style

127. Birkos, Alexander S., and Lewis A. Tambs, eds. *African and Black American studies*. Littleton, CO: Libraries Unlimited, 1975. 205p. *(Academic writer's guide to periodicals,* v. 3.) ISBN 0-87287-109-6; LC card 74-31262. $11.50.

Includes 200 multinational ''periodicals and monograph series that publish at least a portion of their articles in the English language.'' The titles are arranged alphabetically and contain information on the editor, the editorial address, sponsor, frequency, subscription price, year founded, number of subscribers, editorial interest, editorial policies including the name of the style manual required, length of the manuscript, author payment, and notes on special features. Provided are a chronological index, a geographical index, and a topical index.

128. Birkos, Alexander S., and Lewis A. Tambs, eds. *East European and Slavic studies*. [Kent, OH]: Kent State University Press, [1973]. 572p. (*Academic writer's guide to periodicals*, v. 2.) ISBN 0-87738-127-0, ISBN 0-87338-128-9pbk.; LC card 73-158303. $10.00, $7.00pbk.

A high proportion of English-language titles is to be found among the 496 journals about the countries of the Baltic area, Eastern Europe, and the Soviet Union. Each title includes editor, address, sponsor, frequency, editorial interest, and editorial policies, including designation of style manual, if one is recommended. Included are an analytical index, a chronological index, a geographical index, and a topical index.

129. Birkos, Alexander S., and Lewis A. Tambs, eds. *Latin American studies*. [Kent, OH]: Kent State University Press, [1971]. 359p. (*Academic writer's guide to periodicals*, v. 1.) ISBN 0-87338-119-X, ISBN 0-87338-120-3pbk.; LC card 70-160685. $10.00, $7.50pbk.

An alphabetical list of 307 periodicals that publish at least a portion of their articles in English from the following countries: Mexico, Central America, Brazil, the West Indies, and the former Spanish borderlands of North America. Title is followed by the periodical's address and sponsor, frequency, circulation, editorial interest, and policy. The style manual used is specified. Chronological, geographical, and topical indexes are provided.

BIBLIOGRAPHY

General Style

130. Hoffman, Herbert H. *Bibliography without footnotes*. 2nd ed. [Newport Beach, CA]: Headway Publications, 1978. 93p. ISBN 0-89537-013-1. $4.00. (First ed. 1977.)

Divided into 2 major parts. Part 1 includes 7 chapters: 1. structure of documents, 2. parts of bibliographic descriptions, 3. elements of a bibliographic description, 4. title-first style, 5. typographic specifications, 6. split descriptions, and 7. reference notes and *loci*. Part 2 is chapter 8., flow chart and examples. The 3 appendixes are: A. standardized references (*loci classici*) for books of the English Bible, plays of Shakespeare, dialogues of Plato, and works of Aristotle, B. format for a term paper, and C. format for a journal article. The index includes all the examples used in the manual.

Bibliographic style: suggests the collection of citations at the end of a paper in the following order of elements: title, author's last name, author's first name, place, publisher, and date. Derives some support from the flexibility of the *American National Standard for Bibliographic References*. The concepts of levels of bibliographic style for a book or an article presented in the manual are dependent on the standard.

Unorthodox, but interesting presentation of concepts for the placement of endnotes and the compilation of bibliographies.

131. United Nations. Dag Hammarskjöld Library. *Bibliographical style manual.* New York: 1963. vi, 62p. ([Its] *Bibliographical series,* no. 8) ([United Nations. *Document* ST/LIB/ser. B/8.]) LC card 63-2714.

Divided into 7 sections: books and pamphlets, periodicals and newspapers, parts of books, government publications, United Nations documents, League of Nations documents, and abbreviations.

Bibliographic style: derived from North American cataloging manuals, notably the American Library Association's *ALA: Cataloging Rules for Author and Title Entries,* 2nd ed. (Chicago: 1949), the U.S. Library of Congress's *Rules for Descriptive Cataloging in the Library of Congress,* Preliminary ed. (Washington, DC: USGPO, 1949), and *Supplement* 1949–1951 (Washington, DC: USGPO, 1952). Also found useful was Peyton Hurt's *Bibliography and Footnotes: A Style Manual for College and University Students* (Berkeley, CA: University of California Press, 1949). A style not unlike that presented in the United States Library of Congress General Reference and Bibliography Division's *Bibliographical Procedures & Style: A Manual for Bibliographers in the Library of Congress.* Interesting for its discussion of official publications, e.g., laws, legislative publications, constitutions, treaties, and legal materials, and, of course, especially of value for its treatment of League of Nations and United Nations documents. Updated by *Editorial Directives* issued irregularly by the United Nations' Secretariat. Rules for and examples of footnotes, which are condensed from *Editorial Directive ST/CS/Ser.A/14,* are well presented in "How to Cite United Nations Publications," Chapter 20 of Peter I. Hajnal's *Guide to United Nations Organization, Documentation & Publishing for Students, Researchers, Librarians* (Dobbs Ferry, NY: Oceana Publications, 1978), pp. 187–200.

132. United States. Library of Congress. General Reference and Bibliography Division. *Bibliographical procedures & style: A manual for bibliographers in the Library of Congress,* by Blanche Prichard McCrum and Helen Dudenbostel Jones. Washington, DC: For sale by the Superintendent of Documents, USGPO, 1954; reprinted 1966. vii, 133p. LC card 66-60057. $2.05. ["Reprinted . . . with a list of abbreviations" (pp. 119–23).]

An earlier guide, prepared by Mortimer Taube and Helen F. Conover, is found under: U.S. Library of Congress. Committee on Bibliography and Publications. *Manual for bibliographers in the Library of Congress* (Washington, DC: 1944).

The manual is divided into 2 parts. Part 1, bibliographical procedures, includes I. planning the bibliography and II. procedures for preparing the bibliography. Part 2, bibliographical style, has sections on I. books, pamphlets, and other monographic publications, II. documents, and III. serials. The 7 appendixes are: A. abbreviations, alphabetizing, and numerals, B. use of printed catalog cards, C. annotations, D. title, preliminary matter, and makeup, E. preparation of the index, F. bibliographical procedures and techniques: a selected list of references, and G. abbreviations used in bibliographical entries. The index is detailed.

Bibliographic style: derived in part from the format of Library of Congress printed cards, which in turn is based on the cataloging code in current use, and in part on the internal system of bibliographical description used by the Library's staff. In particular, the Library of Congress manual differs markedly from all other style manuals in its use of italics, which highlight transition words such as *"and"* and *"In"* and emphasize corporate bodies such as "Gt. Brit. *Parliament. House of Commons."* Of necessity, the Library of Congress manual must be supplemented by other style manuals and by the changes brought about by the adoption of the *Anglo-American Cataloguing Rules,* 2nd ed.

Although the Library of Congress manual has not been revised, it is nonetheless a valuable aid when compiling a bibliography. The discussion leads the novice step by step through the planning stages and provides many examples for all types of books and periodical articles. Rare books, law materials, music, technical scientific reports, patents, and nonbook materials such as prints, photographs, maps, and sound recordings are not included. Of particular importance is the description of official publications of the United States in the "Documents" section.

133. Van Leunen, Mary-Claire. *A handbook for scholars.* New York: Knopf; distributed by Random House, 1979, c1978. ix, 354p. ISBN 0-394-40904-3, ISBN 0-394-73395-9pbk.; LC card 77-24436. $12.95, $5.95pbk.

"This book is about the mechanical problems that are specific to scholarly publishing. I have tried to avoid overlap with general manuals of style except in the sections on quotation and on scholarly peculiarities. For help with punctuation, spelling, grammar, diction, style, organization, logic, and rhetoric, look elsewhere. For help with citations, quotations, footnotes, references, and reference lists you have come to the right place." Divided into 4 parts: the text, the reference, the reference list, and manuscript preparation, with appendixes on the vita and on the federal documents of the United States. Indexed.

Bibliographic style: the aim of the author is the elimination of bibliographic information in footnotes by "embedding" a bracketed number on the line which refers to an item appearing only in the reference list at the end of the work. In the reference list, the bibliographic information is "columnated" with author, title, and publisher/date on 3 separate lines. Under the third line is placed the numbers relating to the text. Includes a variety of citation forms for books, periodical articles, pamphlets, unpublished works, theses, archival sources, court cases, microforms, and nonbook materials, such as art works, computer programs, and radio and TV programs.

This handbook has provoked both favorable and unfavorable reviews from the scholarly community. Some applaud the need to shorten the documentation of published papers. Others state that the Van Leunen system creates more trouble than it is worth. The concept of embedding bracketed numbers in the text has already been realized by Robert A. Day in his "citation order system" (*see* item 217). However, it is the columnated format of the elements of the citation that appears to be most controversial. While Van Leunen sees a saving of space in the text with her system, she ignores the added lines of type when the information is moved to the reference list. Also, the bulk of this handbook weighs against its adoption even as a guide to footnotes. Van Leunen's *Handbook for scholars* is reviewed by Naomi B. Pascal in her "Four More Enchiridia," *Scholarly Publishing* 10 (July 1979): 351–58, and by Betty Milum in her review in the *Journal of Library History, Philosophy, & Comparative Librarianship* 15 (Jan. 1980): 242–45. This handbook is no substitute for any of the major style manuals. It should be entitled a *Scholar's Guide to Footnotes.*

BIOLOGY

General Style

134. Council of Biology Editors. Style Manual Committee. *Council of Biology Editors style manual: A guide for authors, editors, and publishers in the biological sciences.* 4th ed. [Arlington, VA]: Distributed by the American Institute of Biological Sciences, [1978]. xvii, 265p. ISBN 0-91430-02-6; LC card 78-50755. $16.00. [First edition (1960) and 2nd edition (1964), by Conference of Biological Editors, have title: *Style manual for biological journals;* 3rd edition (1972), by Committee on Form and Style of the Council of Biology Editors, has title: *CBE style manual.*] Bibliography: pp. 231–40.

> Divided into 12 parts: 1. planning the article, 2. writing the article: the first draft and revisions, 3. the final draft, 4. editorial review of manuscripts, 5. manuscript into print, 6. proof correction, 7. indexing, 8. general style conventions, 9. style in special fields: plant sciences, microbiology, animal sciences, chemistry and biochemistry, geography and geology, 10. abbreviations and symbols, 11. word usage, and 12. an annotated bibliography: style manuals and guides; writing, prose style, and word usage; illustration; science dictionaries; metric and other units; and standards: national and international. The index is detailed.

> Bibliographic style: adopts the *American National Standard for Bibliographic References* with the modification of recommending only initials in place of first names of authors.

> The editors encountered some difficulty in presenting "Style in Special Fields." For example, neurophysiology has been omitted "because their conventions have not been established by appropriate agreement within their professional societies, national or international. We hope that all fields of science may some day agree to use the same conventions in style to facilitate communication among all scientists. To that end, we have adopted recommendations from the American Chemical Society, the American Geological Institute, and the American Institute of Physics that are applicable for the needs of authors in biology."

> Includes detailed lists of scientific abbreviations and symbols. Copious examples are used throughout. This is a detailed style manual incorporating the latest in scientific and bibliographic developments.

BOTANY

General Style

135. Australian Systematic Botanical Society. Taxonomic Publication Committee. *[Points that should be considered when writing a taxonomic paper]* N.p.: [1975?]. [1], 8 leaves. [Parts of this style guide are included in verbatim passages in Hansjörg Eichler's *Guidelines for the preparation of botanical taxonomic papers* (*see* item 136). Photocopy of original held by Linnean Society of New South Wales.]

> Divided into 12 unnumbered parts: coverage; titles; abstract; keys including analytical indented, analytical bracketed, and synoptic; descriptions; distribution; specimen citation; synonymy; types; citation of authors' names; citation of journals or books; and dates of publication.

> Bibliographic style: unique. Guidance is given in choosing which bibliographies are to be designated as authorities for establishing authors' names, abbreviating journal titles, and recording dates.

136. Eichler, Hansjörg. *Guidelines for the preparation of botanical taxonomic papers.* [Melbourne]: Commonwealth Scientific and Industrial Research Organization, Australia, 1977. 28p. ISBN 0-643-00220-0. Bibliography: pp. 21–22.

> Includes guidelines for authors, editors, and referees with recommendations for the presentation of taxonomic botanical revisions. Included are sections on observance of the International Code of Botanical Nomenclature, title, authors, abstract, table of contents, headings, keys, names of taxa, citation of authors' names, synonymies, descriptions, indication of types, basionyms, lectotypification, distribution, maps of distribution, lists of specimens examined, location of type and other voucher specimens, other information and notes, citation of references, dates of publication, abbreviations, indexes to collections and scientific names, illustrations, appendixes, acknowledgments, footnotes, pagination, spelling, punctuation and dates, end of manuscript, proof corrections, and reprints. There follows a 5-page list of signs, symbols, and standard abbreviations.

> Bibliographic style: Harvard, with idiosyncracies. For a book, the date is in parentheses followed by a period. The title is in single quotes with the place of publication in parentheses and a final period preceding the parenthesis close. The author attempts to clarify the choice of

sources for abbreviating journal titles. He recommends G. H. M. Lawrence's *B-P-H*. *Botanico-Periodicum-Huntianum* (Pittsburgh, PA: Hunt Botanical Library, 1968).

A concise, well-thought-out presentation of the problems and solutions to publishing botanical taxonomic papers.

BUSINESS

General Style

137. Graves, Harold F., and Lyne S. S. Hoffman. *Report writing*. 4th ed. Englewood Cliffs, NJ: Prentice-Hall, [1965]. viii, 286p. ISBN 0-13-773671-1; LC card 65-11494. $14.95. (First ed. 1929; 2nd ed. 1942; 3rd ed. 1950.) Bibliography: pp. 275–80.

Composed of 7 chapters: 1. the demand for reports, 2. letter and memorandum, 3. the style of the good report, 4. collecting data, 5. planning the report, 6. preparing the manuscript: rhetorical elements, and 7. preparing the manuscript: format. There follows a section of specimen reports. The handbook section follows many of the standards of the American National Standards Institute. Included are rules for abbreviations, capitalization, compounding words, spelling, numbers, and punctuation. The 2 appendixes are: A. the letter of application and B. bibliography of abstracts and indexes. Indexed.

Bibliographic style: unique. Commas separate all elements with no full stop until the end of the entry. Abbreviations are not used. For books, the order is author's last name, full first name, title, place of publication, publisher, and date. For periodical articles, the order is author's last name, first names, title in double quotes, title of journal in italics, volume number using "vol.," pagination, and date.

Report Writing is specifically for those writing business reports. The flow of the text progresses from one series of examples to another. The exercises throughout the book indicate its usefulness as a textbook. The stress laid on primary skills in writing in the first half of the text is simple and encouraging. *Report Writing* could be more useful if the authors would adopt the *American National Standard for Bibliographic References*.

138. Keithley, Erwin M., and Philip J. Schreiner. *A manual of style for the preparation of papers & reports: Business and management applications.* 3rd ed. Cincinnati, OH: South-western Publishing Co., [c1980]. vi, 77, v, 28p. illus. map. ISBN 0-538-05220-1; LC card 79-64576. $5.00. (First edition (1959) and 2nd edition (1971) have title: *A manual of style for the preparation of papers & reports.*) ["Appendix: Model report": v, 28p. (at end).] Includes bibliographical references.

Divided into 10 sections: 1. basic considerations in preparing to write, 2. basic problems of style encountered in writing papers and reports, 3. writing the cover letter and abstract, 4. the report—arranging, editing, typing, and binding, 5. report preliminaries, 6. the body of the report—general, 7. the body of the report—documentation, 8. the body of the report—tables, charts, diagrams, exhibits, and other illustrative materials, 9. the report appendix, and 10. the report bibliography. There follow a model report, the index, and a guide sheet.

Bibliographic style: identical to the style found in *The Chicago Manual of Style*, except for 2 points: for books, Keithley and Schreiner spell out in full the name of the publisher; for articles, they do not use *Chicago's* elided paginations, e.g., pp. 141–49 rather than 141–49. Bibliographic examples are provided for one, 2, 3 and more than 3 authors, editor, 3 editors, author with translator, book in a series, articles in journals and encyclopedias, public documents, ERIC documents, articles in newspapers, pamphlets, theses and dissertations, speeches, and computer materials. Considering the scope of the manual, more examples of the most difficult entries, e.g. articles in periodicals, might have been provided. This edition differs from the first 2 editions in its examples. "In this third edition examples are presented from materials associated with business, management, business communications, and speech communications."

Reduced examples of report pages are used throughout the manual. They are difficult to read.

139. Lesikar, Raymond V. *Report writing for business.* 6th ed. Homewood, IL: R. D. Irwin, 1981. x, 386p., illus. ISBN 0-256-02479-0; LC card 80-84708. $20.95. (First ed. 1961; 2nd ed. 1965; 3rd ed. 1969; 4th ed. 1973; 5th ed. 1977).

Divided into 16 chapters: 1. orientation to business reports, 2. development of report-writing methods, 3. determining the problem and planning the investigation, 4. collecting information: library research, 5. collecting information: primary research, 6. arranging and interpreting information, 7. constructing the outline, 8. constructing the formal report, 9. constructing short and special reports, 10. techniques of readable writing, 11. qualities of effective report writing, 12. physical presentation of a report, 13. mechanics of documentation and bibliography construction, 14. graphic aids for reports, 15. oral reports, and 16. correctness of punctuation and grammar in reporting. The 6 appendixes are: A. a grading checklist for reports, B. statistical techniques for determining sample size and reliability, C. report problems, D. illustrations of types of reports, E. corrections for the diagnostic test, and F. the gunning fog index. Indexed.

Bibliographic style: unique for books, with author's last name, comma, author's first name or initials, comma, title in capitalized italics, comma, publisher, place of publication, date, comma, and pages. The style for periodical articles follows *The Chicago Manual of Style* except that Lesikar adds ''pp.'' and ''vol.'' in the citation.

This extensive manual is arranged like a textbook with sets of questions at the ends of chapters. It is well illustrated with a thorough analysis of the procedures in writing a good business report. The chapter on the mechanics of documentation and bibliography construction might be expanded with more examples that conform to the style of one of the major style manuals.

140. Lewis, Phillip V., and William H. Baker. *Business report writing.* Columbus, OH: Grid, [1978]. xiii, 273p. ISBN 0-88244-084-5; LC card 78-050045. $16.95. Bibliography: pp. 267–70.

Divided into 6 major parts: I. the nature of researching and reporting, II. business research methodology, III. the process of report writing, IV. the process of oral reporting, V. case studies for report writing, and VI. readings. The first 4 parts include 16 chapters: 1. the function of the business report, 2. the importance of business research, 3. the value of reports for management, 4. analyzing, clarifying, and defining the problem, 5. planning methods to be used, 6. preparing the working plan, 7. constructing and using a questionnaire, 8. utilizing interview techniques in data collection, 9. interpreting the information gathered, 10. basic composition of research reports, 11. organizing your report for presentation, 12. visual communication techniques, 13. prefatory and appended sections, 14. a checklist of requirements for writing effective reports, 15. the oral report in business, and 16. how to present an oral report. Indexed.

Bibliographic style: for books and periodical articles, the style is identical to that found in *The Chicago Manual of Style*, except that Lewis and Baker use roman numerals for volumes.

Discussion questions and exercises conclude each chapter. Concise textbook format. Good coverage of tables and graphs. Well printed and easy to use.

141. Moyer, Ruth, Eleanour Stevens, and Ralph Switzer. *The research and report handbook for managers and executives in business, industry, and government.* New York: Wiley [c1981]. viii, 312p. ISBN 0-471-04257-9, ISBN 0-471-04258-7pbk.; LC card 80-18922. $14.95, $8.95 pbk. Bibliography: pp. 304-05.

This handbook is divided into 7 parts, which are subdivided into chapters. Part I, business reports, contains chapters on the introduction to business reports, long reports, and memorandum and letter reports. Part II, special reporting situations, has chapters on legal briefs, minutes, policy statements, procedures, and proposals. Part III, preparing the report, includes chapters on defining the problem, outlining the information, performing the research, preparing the graphic aids, and presenting the information. Part IV, documentation, includes chapters on requirements for documentation, reference notes, first notes, second reference notes, and bibliography. Part V, selected government references for business writers, includes chapters on federal government references, state government references, other government references, and United Nations reference books. Part VI, selected sources of business information, includes indexes to books and periodicals, indexes to articles, directories, dictionaries, services and newsletters, handbooks, general references, compiled sources of legal information, compiled sources of tax information, and computer literature. Part VII, style guide, includes abbreviated forms, capitalization, number usage, and punctuation. Indexed.

Bibliographic style: follows *The Chicago Manual of Style.* Includes examples for books, periodical articles, newspaper articles, brochures, cassettes, computer programs, dictionaries, dissertations, encyclopedias, equipment specifications, film, handbooks, interviews, lectures, letters, microforms, pamphlets, proceedings, radio programs, taped recordings, television programs, unpublished works, and yearbooks.

A well-designed book that is easy to use. Includes sample pages of style throughout the handbook. Good annotated chapters on indexes to books and periodicals; indexes to articles; directories; dictionaries; services and newsletters; handbooks; and reference books. A valuable manual because of its comprehensive treatment of all aspects of style for the businessperson.

Journal Style

142. Kurtz, David L., and A. Edward Spitz. *An academic writer's guide to publishing in business and economic journals.* 2nd ed. Ypsilanti, MI: Eastern Michigan University, Bureau of Business Services and Research, [1974]. 247p.

> Contains over 200 titles, predominantly from the United States, arranged alphabetically with information on: 1. publication, including frequency and circulation, 2. type of manuscript, 3. submission of articles including length, illustrative matter, and style designation (including the name of the style manual where specified), and 4. author information with data on complementary copies and reprints. No index is provided.

CHEMISTRY

General Style

143. American Chemical Society. *Handbook for authors of papers in American Chemical Society publications.* Washington, DC: 1978. vi, 122p. ISBN 0-8412-0425-X, ISBN 0-8412-0430pbk.; LC card 78-6401. $7.50, $3.75pbk. Bibliography: pp. 114–17. (1965 edition has title: *Handbook for authors of papers in the research journals of the American Chemical Society;* 1967 edition has title: *Handbook for authors of papers in the journals of the American Chemical Society.*)

> Divided into 5 parts: American Chemical Society books and journals (there are 23 of the latter), the scientific paper, the manuscript, the editorial process, and a sequence of appendixes on the international system of units (SI), symbols for chemical elements and physico-chemical quantities, preferred spellings, recurring errors, composition procedures, guidelines for preparation and submission of documents to be microfilmed, hints to the typist, and journal abbreviations. The section on the manuscript includes information on style, abbreviations, symbols, units, chemical nomenclature, preparation and presentation of experimental details, microform supplements, miniprint material, tables, illustrations, structural formulas, and a format for documentation of footnotes and references. The section on the editorial process includes data on manuscript review and the processing of accepted manuscripts such as technical editing, author's proof, corrections, reprints, page charges, and liability and copying rights.

Bibliographic style: recommends the use of the *American National Standard for Bibliographic References* to be modified by an editor for a specific book or journal. However, the examples given in the handbook are prestandard and do not demonstrate the adoption of the standard (cf. examples on pp. 73–77).

Good coverage of illustrated material, tables, symbols and abbreviations, and a good index.

EDUCATION

General Style

144. Australian Council for Educational Research. *ACER house style notes*. [Hawthorn, Victoria]: 1978. 28p.

Divided into 16 sections: introduction, abbreviations, acknowledgments, capital initials, contents, index, letters, memorandum, minutes of meetings, numbers, preparation of reports, punctuation, quotations, spelling, test items, and the International System of Units. In areas not covered by the *ACER House Style Notes,* the writer is referred to the *Style Manual for Authors, Editors and Printers of Australian Government Publications (see* item 50).

Bibliographic style: 2 styles with examples are presented. The first is that of the American Sociological Association, and the second is that of the American Psychological Association. Examples are provided for books, periodical articles, doctoral dissertations, and chapters from books.

Primarily for those preparing reports for ACER.

145. Katz, Sidney B., Jerome T. Kapes, and Percy A. Zirkel. *Resources for writing for publication in education.* New York; London: Teachers College Press, Teachers College, Columbia University, 1980. xiii, 130p. ISBN 0-8077-2579-X; LC card 79-27127. $6.50. Bibliography: pp. 111–21.

Its 7 chapters are: 1. the importance of publication, 2. conference and convention papers, 3. journals, 4. books and monographs, 5. indices, 6. style manuals and writing guides, and 7. copyright information. Also included are 5 appendixes: A. American Educational Research Association call for papers at the 1980 annual meeting, B. ERIC clearinghouses and services, C. [20] new journals in education, D.

"Guidelines for nonsexist language in APA journals," reprinted from *Change Sheet 2*, an 8-page supplement dated June 1977 to the *Publication Manual of the American Psychological Association*, 2nd ed. (Washington, DC: 1980, c1974), and E. "fair use" guidelines for classroom copying.

Bibliographic style: discusses and provides examples of 3 styles from the following manuals: *Publication Manual of the American Psychological Association*, *The Chicago Manual of Style*, and the *MLA Handbook for Writers of Research Papers, Theses, and Dissertations*. The chapter on "Style Manuals and Writing Guides" also includes evaluations of the 3 manuals cited above in relation to the field of education. The authors note that "APA style is the most commonly used of the formats specified under 'Education' in the D[irectory of] P[ublishing] O[pportunities]."

This guide is well formatted, the style is concise, and the contents will be of interest to anyone wishing to publish in the field of education. The authors are suggestive in their comments rather than prescriptive.

146. National Education Association of the United States. *NEA style manual for writers and editors*. Washington, DC: 1974. 92p. LC card 74-6142. $3.00 prepaid unless institutional stationery is used in ordering. (Unnumbered editions issued in 1962 and 1966.) (Available by mail only from the Association's Publications Order Department, The Academic Building, Saw Mill Road, West Haven, CT 06516.)

An excellent, concise style manual for the writer or editor working with educational materials. Divided into 16 sections: abbreviations and symbols (especially useful for the acronyms of major educational institutions); capitalization (many examples); dates and time; division of words; foreign words and phrases (for French, Latin, and the use of roman type); italics; lists and enumerations (for typographers); numbers and figures; plurals; punctuation (very detailed with many examples); titles (appellations), generic personal references; tables; bibliographical and footnote references; identification on NEA-produced materials (position of the logotype); title page and reverse; preparing copy for the typesetter; and a detailed index.

Bibliographic style: unique, but relying heavily on that presented in *The Chicago Manual of Style*. Includes notations and examples for abstracts, alphabetizing, anthologies, articles, authors, bibliographies, book reviews, books and pamphlets, census reports, chapters, condensations, Congressional bills, editor statements, editorials, ERIC documents, excerpts, federal laws, films, filmstrips, hearings

(Congressional), joint committee publications, judicial decisions, leaflets, mimeographed publications, monographs, newspaper articles, out of print publications, parts of a book, periodicals, proceedings, publications in a series, places of publication, reprints, revised editions, school publications, speeches, state laws, state publications, supplements to periodicals, surveys, symposia, tests, theses, translations, U.S. Office of Education publications, unpublished material, volume designations, and yearbooks.

A well-balanced style manual with detailed descriptions and copious examples designed not only for teachers, education specialists, and researchers, but also for anyone seeking aid on education topics. The large index allows easy access to subjects otherwise ignored by other manuals.

147. New Zealand Council for Educational Research. *Guide for preparing the manuscript of reports intended for publication.* [Wellington: 197–.] 5 leaves.

" . . . adapted from a number of sources, notably the Chicago University Press, *A Manual of Style.*"

Divided into 11 sections: typing, spelling, foreign words, capitalization, abbreviations, italics, quotations, numbers, dates, tables and figures, and footnotes.

Bibliographic style: modified form adapted from *The Chicago Manual of Style.* Place of publication, publisher, and date of publication are enclosed in parentheses.

148. Scott, Foresman and Co. Editorial Dept. *A style guide.* Glenview, IL: [c1976]. ii, 62p.

"This style guide is intended to provide a ready reference for answers to questions that come up with some frequency in the writing and editing of the materials in the Elhi departments of Scott, Foresman and Company. The guide is based on the elements of style, grammar, and usage discussed in *A Manual of Style,* published by the University of Chicago Press, (1969 ed.); *Writer's Guide and Index to English* by Porter G. Perrin, revised by Wilma R. Ebbit, (1972 ed.); *Reference Handbook of Grammar and Usage,* published by Scott, Foresman and Company, (1972 ed.); *Words into Type* by Marjorie E. Skillin and others (1974 ed.); *The Elements of Style* by William Strunk (1972 ed.); *Functional English for Writers* by Kevin G. Burne and others (1964 ed.); and *Handbook of Current English* by Porter G. Perrin and Jim W. Corder (1975 ed.)."

Divided into 43 sections: abbreviations, abridging and adapting, apostrophe, Bible, bibliographies, brackets, capitalization, colon, comma, copyright notice, corporate name of the company, credit lines, dash, dates, division of words, ellipsis, exclamation point, footnotes, foreign words, glossaries, grammar and usage, hyphen, indexes, italics, listings and outlines, mathematics, numerals, parentheses, period, plays, poems, possessives, printing key, proofreaders' marks, punctuation, question mark, quotation marks, quoted material, semicolon, slant line, spelling, time, and wording. Includes index.

Bibliographic style: follows *The Chicago Manual of Style*. Includes examples for books, periodical articles, films, filmstrips, recordings, and works of art.

Useful as a reference aid because of its dictionary arrangement and its amalgam of various elements from the major style manuals.

Journal Style

149. Arnold, Darlene B., and Kenneth O. Doyle, Jr. *Education/psychology journals: A scholar's guide*. Metuchen, NJ: Scarecrow Press, 1975. 143p. ISBN 0-8108-0779-3; LC card 74-23507. $11.00.

Describes 122 journals of professional interest to psychologists, educationists, educational psychologists, and educators. Excluded journals are those in the areas of mental health, counseling, and psychotherapy.

Each title is arranged alphabetically with the journal's address, information on the publisher and copyright, subscription price, frequency, circulation, pages per issue, description of the journal's goals, article content, intended audience, special features, acceptance/rejection criteria and procedures, manuscript disposition, style requirements including the name of the style manual required, payment, and reprints. A subject index is provided.

150. Beedon, Laurel, and Joseph Heinmiller. *Writing for education journals*. Bloomington, IN: Phi Delta Kappa Educational Foundation, c1979. 38p. (*Fastback,* 136.) ISBN 0-87367-136-8; LC card 79-66532. $0.75pbk. Bibliography: p. 38.

Divided into 6 topics: introduction, the idea, identifying and selecting a publisher, technical requirements for manuscripts, selected directory of education journals, and suggested references.

The "Selected Directory of Education Journals" is an unnumbered annotated list of 28 titles that serves as a sample of education periodicals. It is a useful, short manual that concentrates on both the mechanics of and the ideas behind a published paper.

151. Cameron, Jack R., and William E. Goding. *A guide to publishing in education: An annotated international index of selected journals in education.* Calgary: Foothills Educational Press, Faculty of Education, University of Calgary, 1977. xv, 113p. LC card 79-300509. C$7.00.

This guide contains entries for 165 journals arranged under the following broad subjects: administration; curriculum and instruction including English, fine arts, language, mathematics, science, social studies, and general methods; early childhood; foundations; higher education; inter-disciplinary studies; libraries; media; psychology; reading; research; and special education. "The American and British listings have been limited to a representative cross-section of the most important journals. A large majority of relevant educational publishing in Canada is included. . . ." Canadian titles are asterisked. Each entry includes 1. frequency, 2. approximate circulation, 3. readership, 4. index listings, 5. average length of article, 6. article selection procedures, 7. average time between acceptance and publication, 8. footnote style, 9. author bibliographical data, 10. fields stressed, 11. types of articles published, 12. general contents of majority of articles published, 13. article-related items accepted, 14. book review policy, 15. letters to the editors, and 16. other editorial features. Includes an index of journals cited.

152. Camp, William L., and Bryan L. Schwark. *Guide to periodicals in education and its academic disciplines.* 2nd ed. Metuchen, NJ: Scarecrow Press, 1975. x, 552p. ISBN 0-8108-0814-5; LC card 75-6784. $19.50. [First edition (1968) has title: *Guide to periodicals in education.*]

Includes titles of 602 education and education-related journals published in the United States. Excluded are regional, state, and local publications, alumni magazines, handbooks, student publications, annual reports, transactions and proceedings, college bulletins, and monographs in series. Entries are arranged alphabetically within general categories listed in the table of contents. Each entry provides the editor's address, editorial policy, including the name of the style manual used, if any, and manuscript disposition. The subjects of the education-related journals include art, biology, chemistry and physics, communications, economics, ethnology, health, history, law, libraries, linguistics, mathematics, music, political science, psychology, social work, and sociology. A list of style manuals, a master list of subject headings, a subject index, and a title index are provided.

153. Krepel, Wayne J., and Charles R. DuVall. *Education and education-related serials: A directory.* Littleton, CO: Libraries Unlimited, 1977. 255p. ISBN 0-87287-131-2; LC card 76-47040. $15.00.

Titles of 501 journals and newsletters from Canada and the United States are listed alphabetically. Each entry includes the following information: name of publisher, circulation, frequency, subscription price, indexes, year of first issue, editor's name and address, description of the journal, information on solicited and unsolicited manuscripts and preferred style, including the name of the style manual, reporting time, number of copies, publication lag, payment, theme issues, and copyright. A subject index is provided.

GEOLOGY

General Style

154. Blackadar, Robert G., H. Dumych, and P. J. Griffin, comps. *Guide to authors: A guide for the preparation of geological maps and reports.* [Ottawa: Geological Survey of Canada], 1979. [v], 66p. illus. (Canada. Geological survey. *Miscellaneous report, 29.*) ISBN 0-660-10060-6. C$3.00 Canada, C$3.60 elsewhere.

Divided into 9 unnumbered sections: publications issued by the Geological Survey; the publication process; how to prepare a manuscript geological map; joint authorship; critical review; acknowledgments; metric system; writing a geological report; and aids to writing, including grammar, abbreviations, capitalization, compounding of words, italics, numerical expressions, punctuation, spelling, suggested word usages, and list of prepositions. Indexed.

Bibliographic style: Harvard. Names of journals and periodicals are no longer abbreviated.

Excellent step-by-step manual, well illustrated with copious examples throughout. The guidelines on grammatical usage and bibliographic style are clear and easy to follow.

155. Cochran, Wendell, Peter Fenner, and Mary Hill, eds. *Geowriting: A guide to writing, editing, and printing in earth science.* 3rd ed. Falls Church, VA: American Geological Institute, 1979. 79p. ISBN 0-913312-13-4; LC card 79-50569. $4.00 prepaid. (First ed. 1973; 2nd ed. 1974.) Bibliography (annotated): pp. 65–77.

> Bibliographic style: no bibliographic style is recommended. The extensive bibliography is presented in prose format and might well be overlooked with its title "Digging Deeper."

> Useful for the beginning geologist, who should read the guide rather than use it for reference, because of its poor index. Other style manuals such as Blackadar (*see* item 154) and that issued by the Geological Survey of the United States (*see* item 156), should also be consulted before a paper is begun. Especially useful is the section "Judgment by Peers," which explains the review process both before and after publication.

156. United States. Geological Survey. *Suggestions to authors of the reports of the United States Geological Survey.* 6th ed. Washington, DC: For sale by the Superintendent of Documents, USGPO, 1978. xi, 273p. $6.25. [First edition (1909), 2nd edition (1913), 3rd edition (1916), and 4th edition (1935) have title: *Suggestions to authors of papers submitted for publication by the United States Geological Survey, with directions to typists* (varies slightly); 5th ed. 1958.]

> Includes detailed information on illustrations; matters of style, including references in text and reference lists; proofreading; and special sections on reports on water resources, mineral reserves and resources, stratigraphic nomenclature and description, paleontologic matter, geological reports and the computer, the metric system, and a review of the basics of English. Detailed index.

> Bibliographic style: Harvard. Includes numerous examples of citations for periodical articles, maps, scientific reports, parts of books, and articles in foreign languages with English translation of titles. For additional bibliographic information, the writer is referred to *The Chicago Manual of Style* (*see* item 113) and *Bibliographical Procedures & Style* (*see* item 132), issued by the General Reference and Bibliography Division of the United States Library of Congress.

> Unnumbered chapters and an unordered system of presentation lessen the usefulness of this manual. The detailed index does compensate to a great degree, but a schematic breakdown with clear running heads and subheads would make the manual easier to use. Additional annotated

aids are located at the end of each chapter for follow-up reading. This guide remains a comprehensive manual to publishing geological papers and reports.

HISTORY

General Style

157. Council for British Archaeology. *Notes for authors.* [London?: between 1976 and 1981.] 8p.

Divided into 6 parts: 1. preparation and presentation of typescript, 2. illustrations, 3. bibliographical references, 4. CBA-preferred house style, 5. proofs, and 6. reference works.

Bibliographic style: Harvard, without any periods or full stops.

A complete statement of the Council's style is to be found in *Signposts for Archaeological Publication.*

158. Council for British Archaeology. Publications Committee. *Signposts for archaeological publication: A guide to good practice in the presentation and printing of archaeological periodicals and monographs.* 2nd ed. [London]: 1979. 36p. ISBN 0-900312-93-9; £1.95, plus 15p postage. Bibliography: pp. 20–23.

Divided into 10 unnumbered parts: design, production, estimates, presentation, standardization, deposit copies, sales and possible outlets, copyright law, select bibliography, and a glossary of printing terms in common use. The 2 appendixes are: A. CBA standard list of abbreviated titles of current periodicals and series as of June 1979 and B. CBA notes for authors (abridged). No index is provided.

Bibliographic style: Harvard style as recommended by the Royal Society of London. "One particular problem in archaeology is that journals are sometimes published 'for' a year but have an imprint of a later date. This is to be indicated as follows: *Archaeol J*, **122**, 1965 (1966), ie the imprint date follows in brackets [i.e., parentheses] the 'year for which.' " As "ie" in the above quotation indicates, periods are not used for abbreviations.

Very useful booklet particularly in designating which British standards are to be used in the preparation of an archaeological publication. The unannotated bibliography is arranged by subject: 1. archaeology and publishing, 2. technical processes in printing, 3. the editor's job, 4. directions, 5. preparation of archaeological illustrations, and 6. index preparation.

A concise, well-designed booklet with considerable detail on the publication of periodical articles and books on archaeology.

159. Elrington, C. R., ed. *Handbook for editors and authors [of] the Victoria history of the counties of England.* [London]: University of London, Institute of Historical Research, 1978, [c1970]. 63p. (*The Victoria history of the counties of England.*) ISBN 0-901179-03-5; LC card 70-515451. £1.50.

"This handbook is a revised and enlarged version of the *Handbook for Contributors* issued in 1954. It supersedes all previous instructions about printing styles and abbreviations in the *History* and all relevant parts of the original *Guide,* printed in 1903. Although designed strictly for those to whom it is addressed, it is thought that it might prove useful to others engaged in writing or editing comparable historical works, and therefore it is for the first time published."

"It is based, as all previous V.C.H. guides have been, on *Hart's Rules for Compositors and Readers at the University Press, Oxford.*"

Divided into 4 major parts: 1. printing style in the text, 2. the footnotes, 3. the submission of copy, illustrations, and the correction of proofs, and 4. index and list of abbreviations. Includes lists of English forms of Latin forenames and surnames, frequently cited classes of public records, and abbreviations for frequently cited books, journals, and learned societies' publications. The footnote style is unique and complex.

Bibliographic style: no bibliographic style is presented.

An important guide for anyone doing research in English history.

160. Pontifical Institute of Mediaeval Studies. Department of Publications. *Style sheet.* [Toronto?: 197–?] 5 leaves.

"The Department follows *A Manual of Style,* 12th ed. (Chicago, 1969) with the following additions, exceptions, and recent changes. These points also cover any variants in the *MLA Style Sheet,* 2nd ed. (New York, 1970)."

Bibliographic style: "A bibliography is a standard requirement of PIMS books. The bibliography should ordinarily include all works cited in the text, along with place and date of publication and the publisher's name. The name and date of publication will suffice for works published before 1900. . . . Authors and titles should conform to the Library of Congress cataloguing system." Otherwise, PIMS follows *The Chicago Manual of Style.*

Contains bibliographic examples for the works of Plato and Aristotle, Greek and medieval commentaries on Aristotle, incunabula, medieval manuscripts, and civil and canon law.

161. University of New Mexico Press. *Histories of the American frontier series: Suggestions to authors.* [Albuquerque, NM]: 1976. 12 leaves.

"The series, as planned with the collaboration of some thirty leading authorities, is designed to describe the westward expansion of the American people from the beginning of settlement to the present. . . ." The series was purchased from Holt, Rinehart and Winston in 1973. Suggestions to Authors is divided into 6 parts: *Histories of the American Frontier Series,* purpose of the series, suggested editorial procedure, preparation of the manuscript, maps and illustrations, and style sheet.

Bibliographic style: "The bibliography should be annotated and in essay form. Brief descriptive comments on each book cited should be included. For the proper form to be followed, see bibliographical essays in the published volumes."

An extensive list of names of native American peoples is included.

Journal Style

162. Steiner, Dale R. *Historical journals: A handbook for writers and reviewers.* Santa Barbara, CA: ABC-Clio, [c1981]. x, 213p. ISBN 0-87436-312-8, ISBN 0-87436-337-3 text ed. $28.50, $13.85 text ed.

"First, the *Handbook* offers general suggestions on the preparation and submission of manuscripts. Second, it contains a Directory which lists more than three hundred and fifty journals published in the United States and Canada, and provides specific information on the editorial standards and publishing policies of each."

Useful as a list of current potential publishing outlets for periodical articles on historical topics, the *Handbook* includes information on the journal's focus, international affiliation, name of editor and book review editor, address, frequency, circulation, pages/issue, and readership. Specifics for manuscripts include the need for a query, abstract, the style guide recommended, preferred length, number of copies to be submitted, notes, blind referee, time to consider manuscript, illustrations accepted, and foreign languages. Additional information is provided for reviews. A subject index is included.

HUMANITIES

General Style

163. Canadian Federation for the Humanities. *A guide to scholarly publishing in Canada = Guide de l'édition savante au Canada.* 3rd ed., rev. [Ottawa: Aid to Scholarly Publications Programme] Canadian Federation for the Humanities/Social Science Federation of Canada, [1979]. 117, 79p. (First ed. 1971; 2nd ed. 1973.) Bibliography: pp. 49–54.

> Divided into 3 major sections. Part I. publishing, consists of submitting a manuscript, a note on theses, finding a publisher, evaluations, revisions, costs, production, a note on indices, costing, subsidy, contracts, copyright, book production, other methods of publication and production, and sales and promotion. Part II is an unannotated bibliography of articles and books arranged by subject, e.g., editing, evaluation, general. Part III is a directory of Canadian publishers. Some entries include style requirements.

> Bibliographic style: no bibliographic style is presented. Individual publishers should be consulted for their house styles when they are not indicated in the publishers' directory section.

164. Modern Humanities Research Association. *MHRA style book: Notes for authors, editors, and writers of dissertations.* Edited by A.S. Maney and R.L. Smallwood in consultation with the Committee of the Association. 3rd ed. London: 1981. vi, 75p. ISBN 0-900547-79-0. £2.00, £2.50 outside the U.K. (Available from W. S. Maney & Son Ltd, Hudson Road, Leeds LS9 7DL England.) (First ed. 1971; 2nd ed. 1978.) Bibliography: p. 58.

> "The purpose of this handbook is to assist authors and editors of academic publications, and those preparing dissertations, to achieve clarity and consistency in matters of style and presentation." It is divided into 15 chapters: 1. preparing the manuscript, 2. spelling, 3. abbreviations, 4. punctuation, 5. capitalization, 6. italics, 7. dates, 8. quotations and quotation marks, 9. footnotes, 10. references, 11. presentation of theses and dissertations, 12. glossary, 13. useful works of reference, 14. proof correction, and 15. index.

Bibliographic style: for books, the format is author's last name followed by first name or initials. Titles of books are italicized. Place of publication and date are in parentheses, which may be omitted. For periodical articles, the format is author's last name, first name or initials, article title in single quotes, journal title capitalized in italics, volume number without "vol." designation, date in parentheses, and finally inclusive pagination without "pp." designation. The citation by the "Author-Date system," also called Harvard style or scientific style, is introduced for both footnotes and bibliographies with this edition.

The *MHRA Style Book* is a concise guide to current academic style in the United Kingdom. Its frequent revision ensures its continued wide use.

165. Modern Language Association of America. *MLA handbook for writers of research papers, themes, and dissertations* [by Joseph Gibaldi and Walter S. Achtert]. Student ed. New York: 1980, [i.e. 1982, c1977].[ix], 163p. ISBN 0-87352-000-9 student ed., ISBN 0-87352-450-0 reference ed.; LC card 77-76954. $5.65pbk. [First edition (1951) and 2nd edition (1970) have title: *MLA style sheet*. First (1977), 2nd (1978), 4th (1980), and 5th (1982) printings also called "student edition"; 3rd printing (1979) also called "reference edition."]

"Based on William Riley Parker's *The MLA Style Sheet* (1951), as revised in 1970 by John H. Fisher and others, the *MLA Handbook for Writers of Research Papers, Theses, and Dissertations* reflects the thinking and incorporates the suggestions of teachers, scholars, and students throughout the United States and Canada." The handbook is arranged in 6 sections: research and writing, mechanics of writing, preparing the manuscript, documentation, bibliography, and abbreviations and reference words. The appendix covers the preparation of theses and dissertations. A detailed index is followed by sample pages of a research paper with spacing clearly indicated.

Bibliographic style: applies only to bibliographies of research papers. For a book, the elements are author's last name, first name, period, title in italics, period, place, colon, publisher (abbreviated where possible), comma, and date of publication. For a periodical article, author (last name first), title of the article in double quotation marks, name of the periodical italicized and abbreviated where possible, volume number without "vol.," date in parentheses, comma, and inclusive pagination. In addition to books and periodical articles, sample citations are provided for pamphlets, government publications, legal references, letters to the editor, signed and unsigned reviews, lectures, films, theatrical performances, works of art, radio and TV programs, sound recordings, personal letters, and interviews. Generally, this manual is not used by the scientific community, which prefers manuals in their respective disciplines, or perhaps the *American National Standard for Bibliographic References*.

The *MLA Handbook* is the major style manual for the humanities in the United States. Its own list of other style manuals (pp. 95–96) is now out of date. Reviewed in Naomi B. Pascal's "Four More Enchiridia," *Scholarly Publishing* 10 (July 1979): 351–58.

166. Wiles, Roy M. *Scholarly reporting in the humanities.* 4th ed., rev. Toronto: Published in association with the Humanities Research Council of Canada by University of Toronto Press, [1977, c1970]. x, 58p. ISBN 0-8020-1497-6; LC card 68-102276. C$3.00. ["The First and Second Editions (dated 1951 and 1958) were issued by the Humanities Research Council of Canada." Third ed. 1961; 4th ed. 1968.] Bibliography: pp. 51–53.

Divided into 4 parts: I. general format of typescript, II. footnotes, III. bibliography, and IV. selected references. Indexed.

Bibliographic style: identical to that presented in the *MLA Handbook for Writers of Research Papers, Theses, and Dissertations*. A lengthy discussion on the preparation of a bibliography is included. Examples of entries for books, pamphlets, articles, parts of books, manuscripts, and typescripts are provided.

"This treatise on the form of scholarly reports in the humanities has been prepared as an aid to Canadian research workers using the English language in their writing." A pragmatic manual providing a step-by-step procedure for writing a research paper in the humanities.

LAW

General Style

167. *House style: The preparation and printing of books for Sweet & Maxwell/Stevens & Sons, W. Green & Son.* London: Sweet & Maxwell, 1975. 115p.

Divided into 6 parts: guidance for authors and editors, citation of authorities, prelims and indexes, miscellaneous, alphabetical index to house style, and specimen type faces. In the section "Citation of

Authorities,'' is extensive treatment of legal periodicals, cases, and legislation for the governments of the United Kingdom. Cases also include information for Ireland, Australia, Canada, India, New Zealand, and the U.S. Also included are a section on international and world organization material and a section on European material, in particular France, Germany, the Soviet Union, Switzerland, and the Common Market.

Bibliographic style: follows citation style. Title, separated from inverted author's name by a comma, is italicized. Imprint, omitting place and publisher, is enclosed within parentheses. Citations in periodicals and serials follow legal style as laid out in ''Citation of Authorities.''

The most useful legal style manual issued in the United Kingdom. Particularly valuable for citations to Commonwealth and European legal materials. ''In the case of international and European materials the American practice, as set out in The Harvard Law Review Association's *A Uniform System of Citation* (10th ed., 1958), has in many cases been followed, transatlantic conformity seeming possible in this field at least.''

168. Illinois. Supreme Court. *Style manual for Illinois Supreme Court.* Stephen D. Porter, reporter of decisions. [Springfield, IL]: 1977. 21, [15] leaves.

Includes 19 sections on: 1. the opinion, 2. title of opinion and designation of parties, 3. citation of cases, 4. citation to constitutions, 5. citation to statutes, 6. periodicals, 7. Supreme Court rules, 8. books and other secondary materials, 9. quotations and omitted language, 10. capitalization, 11. compound words, 12. numerals, time, and dates, 13. typeface, 14. spelling, 15. footnotes, 16. other matters of style, 17. final orders, 18. press releases, and 19. matters affecting the filing and publication of opinions. Supplemented by 15 pages photocopied from the current *Style Manual* of the U.S. Government Printing Office.

Bibliographic style: follows citation style, pp. 3–9 and carefully lays out Illinois Supreme Court requirements.

Concise manual noting the court style and its applications to all legal materials.

169. Ohio Northern University Law Review. *Style manual.* [Ada, OH: 1980?] 80p. (Table of contents and index wanting in earlier printings.)

Divided into 3 major parts: I. research, preparation, and writing, II. grammatical composition, and III. technical composition. Research, preparation, and writing includes types of law review articles, style points, footnotes, plagiarism: be on guard, and publishable quality— "PQ." Grammatical composition includes mechanics and punctuation, suggested composition aids, and proofreader's marks. Technical composition consists of case names; reports; briefs and records; constitutions; statutes; bills and resolutions; rules; books and pamphlets; letters, speeches, and interviews; periodicals; newspapers; repeating citations: *Id., Supra, Infra, Hereinafter;* citation of pages and footnotes; subdivision abbreviations; introductory signals; parentheticals; order within a given signal; titles of judges; words or phrases of foreign derivation; and spacing.

Bibliographic style: no bibliographic style is presented.

"The primary purpose of the Style Manual is to insure the uniformity of articles within the Ohio Northern University Law Review."

170. Texas Law Review. *Manual on style*. 4th ed. Austin, TX: c1979. vi, 70p. (2nd ed. 1967.)

Divided into 8 chapters: capitalization, grammar, italics, punctuation, quotations, spelling, preparation of the manuscript, and miscellaneous. The latter includes titles of persons, names of companies, and numbers. A good index makes the manual easy to use.

Bibliographic style: no bibliographic style is presented.

171. *A Uniform system of citation.* 13th ed. [Cambridge, MA: Harvard Law Review Association, 1982] c1981. xii, 237p. LC card 41-12137; $4.00.

Called also *"Harvard blue book."*

"This book has three basic parts. The first (rules 1–9) includes general rules of citation and style. It is intended to serve as a self-contained introduction to principles of legal citation. . . . The second part (rules 10–19) collects technical rules of citation relating to cases, statutes, periodicals, and other specific forms of authority. . . . The final part (tables) contains lists—divided by country and state—of reporters, codes, sessions laws, and other sources, and their abbreviations." A tabular alphabetical arrangement of rules and tables has been introduced with this edition: A. general rules of citation and style, B. cases, C. constitutions, statutes, and legislative, administrative, and executive materials, D. books, pamphlets, unpublished materials, periodicals, newspapers, E. services, F. international materials, G. tables: United States, and H. tables: foreign, including Australia and its states and territories, Canada and its provinces and territories, India, New

Zealand, United Kingdom and its divisions, Argentina, Brazil, France, German Democratic Republic, Federal Repbulic of Germany and its states, Italy, Japan, Mexico, the Netherlands, roman law, and Switzerland and its cantons. Section I is a detailed index to instructions and examples.

Bibliographic style: contrasting typefaces are provided in citation forms for briefs and memoranda on endpaper and for law review footnotes on p. 1.

The larger format of this edition provides for the tabular arrangement of material heretofore run together in paragraph style. Readability has been considerably improved. Also, changes in the 13th edition are clearly laid out on p. v.

A Uniform System of Citation is especially useful for its extended list of periodical abbreviations and its numerous examples. The system presented is complex and requires thorough attention before it is used. This manual is considered the first authority for the citation of legal materials in the United States.

172. Witkin, Bernard E., and William Nankervis, Jr. *California style manual: A handbook of legal style for California courts and lawyers: Based on California style manual.* 2nd rev. ed. by Robert E. Formichi. North Highlands, CA: [c1977]. xviii, 213p. LC card 77-150076. $5.10. (First published 1942; rev. ed. 1961.) (Available from the Department of General Services, Publications Section, P.O. Box 1015, North Highlands, CA 95660.)

Prefatory material includes a table of abbreviations, author's proofreading rules, and printer's marks for use in correcting proof. The 6 chapters are: I. capitalization, II. citations, III. punctuation, IV. miscellaneous rules, V. title of case, and VI. editorial information. The index is very detailed.

Bibliographic style: follows citation style which is detailed and comprehensive. Although designed for the California courts and lawyers, the *California Style Manual* also includes sections on citations to federal statutes; the internal revenue code; Congressional bills and resolutions; Congressional reports, documents, hearings, debates, and addresses; treaties and international agreements; agency documents; federal administrative rules; regulations and decisions; federal court rules; executive orders and presidential proclamations; and the *United States Code Congressional and Administrative News.*

Very useful because it is the most detailed legal style manual available in the United States. It is up to date and could serve as a national style manual if the national data were separated from that of California.

Journal Style

173. Mersky, Roy M., Robert C. Berring, and James K. McCue, eds. *Author's guide to journals in law, criminal justice, & criminology.* New York: Haworth Press, [c1979]. xvii, 243p. (*Author's guide to journals series.*) ISBN 0-917724-06-2; LC card 78-18805. $24.95.

The preface consists of sections on abstracting, indexing, and bibliographic services included, style manual abbreviations, and an alphabetical list of journals covered. There follows an introduction with an essay on the history of the development of the legal journal in the United States entitled "A Brief Look at Legal Periodicals, and Periodicals in Criminal Law and Criminal Justice." The essay is very well documented. The bulk of the bibliography is 4 separate listings, each arranged alphabetically by title: general law school law reviews, specialized law school law reviews, association publications, and commercial publications. Indexed by subject, title, and keyword. Each unnumbered entry includes title, manuscript address, types of articles and specialized subject areas, journal affiliation, copyright holder, review period, publication time, early publication option, acceptance rate, number of manuscript copies, style sheet supplied, style requirements, subscription address, annual subscription rate, where the journal is indexed/abstracted, circulation, authorship restrictions, inappropriate topics, symposium issues, surveys of laws, reprint policy, page charges, author renumeration, and frequency.

"The *Guide* is intended to assist the prospective author in deciding on an appropriate journal to which to submit his/her article by providing as much information as possible about the journals and their policies." About 417 journals are represented in the listings.

An important reference work that would have been easier to use if there were only one list of citations in place of 4.

LITERATURE

Journal Style

174. *Directory of periodicals publishing articles on English and American literature and language.* 4th ed. Chicago: Swallow Press, [c1974]. [vi], 234p. ISBN 0-8040-0675-X, ISBN 0-8040-0676-8pbk.; LC card 74-21506. $10.00, $3.50pbk. (First ed. 1959; 2nd ed. 1965; 3rd ed. 1970.)

The scope covers "folklore and linguistic periodicals and those journals which might be of interest in the history of ideas, . . . several periodicals in the modern foreign languages, . . . several of the film journals and a sampling of 'little magazines' that carry occasional critical articles."

Includes approximately 660 periodicals arranged alphabetically by title. Each entry contains information on address, year founded and sponsor, major fields of interest, manuscript information, including length, style manual to be used, and time for editorial review, as well as payment and copyright information. Subject indexed.

Titles chosen represent Australia, Canada, India, Ireland, the United Kingdom and the United States, with a selection from other European and Latin American countries.

175. Harmon, Gary L., and Susanna M. Harmon. *Scholar's market: An international directory of periodicals publishing literary scholarship.* Columbus, OH: Ohio State University Libraries, Publications Committee, 1974. xx, 703p. ISBN 0-88215-033-2; LC card 73-620216. $14.50.

Divided into 11 subjects: I. single and multiple author periodicals, II. age and/or nationality, III. genres, IV. American ethnic minorities, V. folklore, VI. film, VII. specialized topics and interdisciplinary studies, VIII. teaching about literature, IX. literary reviews, X. general reviews, and XI. bibliographical and library resources. The 2 appendixes are: A. publishing conventions for manuscript submissions and B. reprint companies most often cited and microfilm and microfiche companies. An author index and a title index are provided.

This is a "guide to periodicals that publish articles in English about literature. . . ." The volume covers 848 English-language periodicals, and each entry contains the following information: title, editorial address, subscription address, frequency, cost, contents, manuscript information, style requirements, copyright holder, reporting time, publication time lag, payment, disposition of rejected manuscripts, information on date of first issue, and information on back issues.

MATHEMATICS

General Style

176. American Mathematical Society. *A manual for authors of mathematical papers.* [7th ed.] Providence, RI: 1980, [c1962]. 20p. $1.00. [First edition published in the *Bulletin* of the American Mathematical Society, v. 68, no. 5 (Sept. 1962); 2nd ed. 1966; 3rd ed. 1970; 4th ed. 1971; 5th ed. 1973; 6th ed. 1978.]

Divided into 22 sections: introduction, organizing a paper (for beginners), limitations of keyboarding, selecting notation, the use of indices, alternatives to expensive notation, mathematical expressions and displays, diagrams and illustrations, matrices and tables, footnotes, bibliography, typing and mimeographing, handwritten symbols, calling for special type and symbols, altering type and copy, proofreading, publications of the American Mathematical Society, instructions for authors of papers for American Mathematical Society publications, publication charges, reprints and price lists, copying rights, and copyright transfer agreement. Table 3 includes a list of 180 signs and special characters.

Bibliographic style: "Items in the bibliography are usually ordered alphabetically by name of author, and they are numbered consecutively. The names of journals should be abbreviated . . . A full list of standard abbreviations can be found in the annual indexes to *Math. Reviews*. The name of the journal is followed in order by the volume number [in bold face], the year [in parentheses], and the first and last page numbers."

"A reference to a book should give in order author, title, edition (if not the first), name of series and number (if one of a series), publisher (or distributor), city, and year. . . ."

A Manual for Authors of Mathematical Papers is a concise reference aid especially useful for its alternatives to expensive notation and its advice on the essential parts of a paper for publication.

177. Bell Telephone Laboratories, Inc. *The preparation and typing of mathematical manuscripts.* 3rd rev. ed. [Murray Hill, NJ]: c1979. 61p.

Divided into 4 parts: 1. preparation of manuscripts, 2. guide for mathematical typing, which includes information on equations, punctuation of equations, special symbols, spacing of mathematical symbols, superscripts, subscripts, fractions, and dividing equations between lines, 3. mathematical symbols and special characters, including information on enclosures, assertions, operations, other symbols, Greek alphabet, script alphabet, transfers, and a glossary of terms, and 4. a Greek and mathematical symbol guide for typing manuscripts.

Bibliographic style: no bibliographic style is presented.

Detailed demonstration and lucid explanation of the preparation of mathematical manuscripts for the typewriter. This guide is especially useful for its copious examples not found elsewhere.

178. Chaundy, T. W., P. R. Barrett, and Charles Batey. *The printing of mathematics: Aids for authors and editors and rules for compositors and readers at the University Press, Oxford.* London: Oxford University Press, [1965]. ix, 109p. illus. ISBN 0-19-711416-4; LC card A55-4625. $4.00. (First published 1954.)

Divided into 3 major parts: I. the mechanics of mathematical printing: "a simple explanation of the technique of printing which is addressed to mathematical authors so that they may understand how their writings are transformed to the orderliness of the printed page"; II. recommendations to mathematical authors, which includes the following sections: 1. introduction, 2. fractions, 3. surds, 4. superiors and inferiors, 5. brackets, 6. embellished characters, 7. displayed formulae, 8. notation (miscellaneous), 9. headings and numbering, 10. footnotes and references, 11. varieties of type, 12. punctuation, 13. wording, 14. preparing copy, 15. correction of proofs, and 16. final queries and offprints; and III. rules for the composition of mathematics at the University Press, Oxford. The 3 appendixes are: A. legible handwriting, B. type specimens and list of special sorts, and C. abbreviations. Indexed.

Bibliographic style: "For an article give the author's initials and name, the title of the article (if desired) in [single] quotation marks, the name of the periodical in italics followed by the number of the series (if any) in brackets, the volume-number (but not part-volume number), the year in brackets, and, finally, the first and last page-numbers of the article. For a book give the author's initials and name, the title of the book in italics, the place and year of publication (or the edition) in brackets. . . . The foregoing scheme is that which appeals generally to the 'pure' mathematician and is followed in detail by such journals as the *Quarterly Journal of Mathematics* (Oxford) and the *Proceedings of the London Mathematical Society*."

A scholarly enterprise that would profit any mathematician thinking about publishing.

179. Stewart, Dorothy G. *A guide to the typing of mathematical notation.* [Santa Monica, CA]: Rand Corporation, 1964, [c1965]. vii, 55p. Photocopy. ([Rand Corporation. *Paper.*] P-3090.) $5.00. Bibliography: p. 55.

Divided into 5 parts: 1. introduction, 2. symbols, 3. fractions, 4. spacing, and 5. arrangement of equations. The 2 appendixes contain A. Mathematical terms and symbols and B. the Greek alphabet. Bibliographic style: no bibliographic style is presented.

A detailed guide to solving the problems of transferring mathematical manuscript to typed copy. The rules presented are flexible for application to the individual problem.

180. Swanson, Ellen. *Mathematics into type: Copy editing and proofreading of mathematics for editorial assistants and authors.* [Rev. ed.] Providence, RI: American Mathematical Society, [1979]. x, 90p. $8.00. (First ed. 1971.) Bibliography: pp. 83–85.

Divided into 9 chapters: 1. especially for authors; 2. how to mark mathematical manuscripts; 3. mathematics in print; 4. techniques of handling manuscript and proof; 5. processing a publication in mathematics; 6. publication style; 7. composition trends; 8. an appendix with seven parts: (1) alternatives to expensive notation, (2) a manuscript after copy-editing, (3) a list of special fonts used in mathematics, (4) signs used in correcting proof, (5) use of proofreading signs, (6) German and script alphabets, and (7) information sheet for printers; and 9. a glossary of "both technical printing terms and mathematical terms."

Bibliographic style: unique, but flexible.

"In the first edition which was published in 1971 it was assumed that typesetting was by the Monotype system. At that time several kinds of composition, including phototypesetting, were in use for mathematics but the bulk was still done by Monotype. By 1979 this has changed dramatically and the bulk of mathematics is composed by phototypesetting, whether it be with or without the use of a computer. The second edition has been revised to reflect this change in composition methods." This manual presents a thorough, concise coverage of the essential points needed by authors and editors to publish books and articles from mathematical manuscripts.

MEDICINE

General Style

181. American Physical Therapy Association. *Style manual: Physical Therapy; Journal of the American Physical Therapy Association.* 4th ed. [Washington, DC]: 1976. 34p. $2.00. Bibliography: p. 30.

Composed of 4 major parts: manuscripts; style; manuscript preparation, submission, and publication; and journal departments, which are further subdivided into 22 numbered topics: 1. types of manuscript, 2. parts of a manuscript, 3. abbreviations, 4. capitalization, 5. correct usage, 6. figures, 7. footnotes, 8. italics, 9. numbers, 10. punctuation, 11. references, 12. spelling, 13. tables, 14. units of measure, 15. manuscript preparation, 16. submission, 17. review, 18. publication and publication rights, 19. physical therapy news, 20. opinions and comments, 21. abstracts of current literature, and 22. book reviews.

Bibliographic style: while the abbreviations of journal titles follow *Index Medicus,* the style does not conform to either *Index Medicus* or the Vancouver declaration.

182. Barclay, William R., M. Therese Southgate, and Robert W. Mayo. *Manual for authors & editors: Editorial style & manuscript preparation.* 7th ed. Compiled for the American Medical Association. Los Altos, CA: Lange Medical Publications, c1981. v, 184p. ISBN 0-87041-243-4; LC card 81-83310. $8.50. (2nd ed. 1963; 3rd ed. 1965; 4th ed. 1966; 5th ed. 1971; 6th ed. 1976.)

Divided into 4 parts. Part 1, specific parts of the text, consists of general organization, titles, by-line and supplementary information, report of cases, data, synopsis-abstract, subheadings, unnumbered footnotes, acknowledgment, addendum and appendix, and references. Part 2, preparing the manuscript, includes presentation and composition, some special matters of usage, editing, style, usage, equipment, manuscript preparation, checking references, *Cumulated Abridged Index Medicus,* tables, illustrations, legends, running heads, page numbering, letter of transmittal, mailing, *Uniform Requirements* [not included], National Auxiliary Publications Service, copyright, consents for photographs, informed consent, and International System of Units (SI Units). Part 3, editorial style, contains abbreviations, accents/diacritics, capitalization, Greek letters, mathematical composition, nomenclature, numbers, percent, plurals, punctuation, statistics, units of measure, and usage. Part 4, manuscript preparation, consists of by-lines, footnotes/annotations, legends, references, running feet/heads, tables, titles, subtitles, and typography. Also included are an appendix of copyediting marks, a copyediting sample, proofreader's marks, and a proofreading sample. The index is detailed.

Bibliographic style: unique to *The Journal of the American Medical Association* and the Association's specialty journals. The AMA style does not conform to the *Uniform Requirements for Manuscripts Submitted to Biomedical Journals,* nor to the *American National Standard for Bibliographic References* used by *Index Medicus.*

This is a very detailed, prescriptive manual employing the latest medical references sources. It includes a useful list of clinical, technical, and general terms with corresponding abbreviations (pp. 46–52).

183. Calnan, James, and Andras Barabas. *Writing medical papers: A practical guide.* London: Heinemann Medical, [1977, c1973]. vii, 121p. illus. ISBN 0-433-05005-5; LC card 73-593841. £2.50, $10.00. Bibliography: pp. 113–16.

Topics in chapters 1–3 include 1.1 writing an examination paper, 1.2 applying for a post, 1.3 a case report, 1.4 a letter to a journal, 1.5 which journal? 1.6 sending it to the editor, 1.7 proofs, printer's corrections, 1.8 readability, 1.9 style, 1.10 in defence of writing, 2.1 writing reports, 2.2 a medical report (for litigation), 2.3 applying for research funds, 2.4 reporting research to the fund donor, 2.5 publishing research, 2.6 synopsis for a learned society, 2.7 speaking after the publication, 2.8 publishing after the lecture, 2.9 consulting the library, 2.10 co-authors, 3.1 coaching, 3.2 reporting a conference, 3.3 an editorial, 3.4 reviewing a book, 3.5 a thesis, and 3.6 a monograph. Topics in chapters 4–7 are devoted to writing the paper: 4.1 the ground plan and flow chart, the title, 4.2 assembly, 4.3 illustrations, 4.4 introduction, 4.5 main data and results, 4.6 discussion, the rules of evidence, 4.7 concluding, 4.8 summary or abstract, 4.9 acknowledgments, 5.1 the first draft, 5.2 the first revision: revising the form, 5.3 punctuation and paragraphs, 5.4 clarity, 5.5 brevity, 5.6 interest, 5.7 jargon, 5.8 rules for numbers, 5.9 having it typed, 6. the 10 commandments, 7.1 references to papers, and 7.2 references to books.

Bibliographic style: Harvard. This guide was published and reprinted before the publication and adoption of the *Uniform Requirements for Manuscripts Submitted to Biomedical Journals* on February 5, 1979.

A common-sense pocketbook whose motto is "it is not so much the value of the work but the manner of presenting it." Informally discusses the problems of writing and publication. Well illustrated with humorous drawings by Barabas.

184. Fishbein, Morris. *Medical writing: The technic and the art.* 4th ed. Springfield, IL: Thomas, [1972]. xi, 203p. illus. ISBN 0-398-02279-8; LC card 73-165883. $13.75. (First ed. 1938; 2nd ed. 1948; 3rd ed. 1957.)

Divided into 17 chapters: 1. an acceptable paper, 2. style, 3. the subject and the material, 4. construction of the manuscript, 5. words and phrases, 6. spelling, 7. capitalization, 8. abbreviations, 9. numbers, 10. pharmaceutic products and prescriptions, 11. bibliographic material, 12. preparation of the manuscript, 13. illustrations, 14. tables and charts, 15. revision of the manuscript, 16. proofreading, and 17. indexing. Indexed.

Bibliographic style: "References are grouped at the end of a paper in the form of a bibliography only when an exhaustive review of the literature has been made on a subject of sufficient importance to warrant such a survey. The references constituting a bibliography may be arranged either alphabetically or chronologically, or in exceptional instances according to some other logical scheme."

The chapters on illustrations, and tables and charts are detailed. The prescribed format for references is superseded by the *Uniform Requirements for Manuscripts Submitted to Biomedical Journals.* A useful reference book, but out of date for references and bibliographic citations.

185. Garn, Stanley. *Writing the biomedical research paper.* Springfield, IL: Thomas, [1970]. vii, 65p. ISBN 0-398-00648-2; LC card 75-97545. Out of print.

Divided into 20 chapters: I. introduction, II. structuring the research report, III. a good title, IV. the authors and identification, V. the abstract, VI. the introduction, VII. methods and materials, VIII. the findings, IX. the discussion, X. bibliography and references, XI. tables, XII. line illustrations, XIII. photographic illustrations, XIV. legends, XV. acknowledgments, XVI. footnotes, XVII. mailing the manuscript out, XVIII. the review process, XIX. reading and returning the proof, and XX. reprints. No bibliography or index is provided.

Bibliographic style: raises the question of variations in style, but does not present any systematic approach to bibliographic references. Out of date in regard to the adoption of the *Uniform Requirements for Manuscripts Submitted to Biomedical Journals* and the examples in *Index Medicus,* which now conform to the *American National Standard for Bibliographic References.*

No examples are offered in this pragmatic guide that follows no prescribed style.

186. International Steering Committee of Medical Editors. *Uniform requirements for manuscripts submitted to biomedical journals.* (The Vancouver declaration, revised.)

Also called "Vancouver style" and the "Uniform requirements." "The material in this document will be revised at intervals. Inquiries and comments originating in North America should be sent to Edward J. Huth, MD, *Annals of internal medicine,* 4200 Pine Street, Philadelphia, PA 19104; those originating in other regions should be sent to Stephen Lock, MA, MB, *British medical journal,* British Medical Association, Tavistock Square, London WC1H 9JR, United Kingdom."

Published in the following journals and separately as a pamphlet:

1. *American review of respiratory disease* 119 (Jan. 1979): 3–10.

2. *Annals on internal medicine* 90 (Jan. 1979): 95–99.

3. *British medical journal* 6162 (Feb. 24, 1979): 532–35. (At head of title: Style matters.)

"Reprints of these instructions will be available to editors of biomedical journals free of charge to authors at a cost of 50p (including postage) from the Editor, *BMJ.* A full list of all participating journals will be published later this year" (See next item).

4. *The Lancet* 8113 (Feb. 24, 1979): 428–31. (At head of title: The Vancouver Style.) Appended: "Notes for Lancet Authors," pp. 430–31 on matters not covered by the requirements.

Includes a summary of requirements, preparation of the manuscript, title page, abstract and keywords, text, acknowledgments, references, tables, illustrations, legends for illustrations, abbreviations, and submission of manuscripts. Appendix 1 contains a tentative list of 19 participating journals. Appendix 2 contains commonly approved abbreviations of terms, symbols, and names of frequently cited journals.

Bibliographic style: "Use the form of references adopted by the US National Library of Medicine and used in *Index Medicus.* . . . The titles of journals should be abbreviated according to the style used in *Index Medicus.* A list of abbreviated names of frequently cited journals is given in Appendix 2; for others, consult the 'List of Journals Indexed,' printed annually in the January issue of *Index Medicus.*"

187. Lea and Febiger, Philadelphia. *Manuscript preparation.* [3rd ed.] Philadelphia, PA: [197–, c1973]. 29p. [First edition (1965) with title: *Manuscript preparation and book publication;* 2nd ed. 1973.] (Stamped on verso of t.p.: "This is the third edition of this booklet, but only the last two editions have been copyrighted.")

Divided into 22 sections: preliminary material; estimate of book size; the outline; headings; matters of style; write, rewrite, and rewrite again; typing of material; acknowledgments; footnotes; cross references; borrowed material; references; illustrations; shipping; manuscript, galley proof, page proof; mechanics of making corrections; author's alterations; copyright; the contributor work; new editions from available type; indexing; and history of the firm.

Bibliographic style: unique. Elements, in order, are author's surname, initials only for forename, colon, title, edition, place of publication, publisher, and date. For periodical articles, abbreviations of periodical titles conform with those in *Index Medicus*.

Concise, useful style manual by one of the major medical publishers in the United States.

188. Library Association. Medical Section. *Reference citation recommendations*. London: 1972. 5p.

". . . in view of the preferred new recommendations for the Vancouver Style, no revision of the recommendations [will] be made." (letter to the compiler dated Dec. 10, 1982).

Bibliographic style: Harvard. Gives examples for books, periodical articles, contributions to symposia and congress proceedings. Recommends the journal title abbreviation system adopted for *Index Medicus*. For later information, *see* the Vancouver declaration, revised (item 186).

189. Year Book Medical Publishers. Editorial Department. *Author's guide*. Prepared by the Editorial and Production Departments. Chicago: [1970]. 29p. illus. ISBN 0-8151-9762-4; LC card 73-138936.

Divided into 6 unnumbered parts: what kind of medical book are you writing?; general considerations; sales and advertising; manuscript preparation, which includes bibliographic material, chapter headings, text headings, reduced type, tables, permission to reprint, references in text to tables and figures, and corrections on galley and page proof; illustrations, including photographs, drawings, graphs and charts, combining several illustrative media; and a summary. The appendix contains 5 illustrations.

Bibliographic style: although designated "Bibliographic Material," the section actually concentrates on footnote style. Citations in the text are enclosed within parentheses. "Bibliographies appearing at the end of chapters should be numbered from 1 up, starting with each chapter. All lists and bibliographies should be typed *double spaced*.

"For all journal abbreviations, follow the style of the *Quarterly Cumulative Index Medicus.*" Current practice is found in the *Uniform Requirements for Manuscripts Submitted to Biomedical Journals.*

A short, well-designed and well-illustrated guide to medical book publishing.

Journal Style

190. Ardell, Donald, and John Y. James. *Author's guide to journals in the health field.* New York: Haworth Press, [1980]. xxxii, 139p. ([*Author's guide to journals series.*]) ISBN 0-917724-09-7; LC card 80-13403. $19.95.

The prefatory material includes abbreviations used for abstracting and indexing services and for style manuals. Included are a list of style manual publishers, a format of journal information, a list of preferred content areas, a sample questionnaire, and an essay on "optimizing article publication in health field journals." The core of the bibliography is 261 titles. Subject, title, and keyword indexes.

Each unnumbered entry includes the journal title, the manuscript address, subscription address, annual subscription rate, where it is indexed/abstracted, circulation/frequency, types of articles, preferred content areas, number of manuscript copies, review period, publication lag time, early publication option, acceptance rate, authorship restrictions, page charges, style requirements, style sheet, revised theses, student papers, and reprint policy. Includes "journals which published articles covering a range of topics in other than purely 'clinical' areas. . . ." Most journals chosen are published in the United States with a few titles from Canada and Switzerland.

More detail on style is in *Information to Authors, 1980–1981: Editorial Guidelines Reproduced from 246 Medical Journals* (*see* item 191).

191. *Information to authors, 1980–1981: Editorial guidelines reproduced from 246 medical journals.* Compiled by Harriet R. Meiss and Doris A. Jaeger. Baltimore, MD; Munich: Urban and Schwarzenberg, 1980. xxx, 665p. ISBN 0-8067-1251 (Baltimore), ISBN 3-541-7151-1 (Munich); LC card 80-19712. $26.00. (Earlier edition 1976). [Supplemented in part by "uniform requirements for manuscripts submitted to biomedical journals: list of participating journals" issued by the International Steering Committee of Medical Editors. (*see* item 192)].

The journals selected are clinical in scope, and the volume "features an exact reproduction of each journal's masthead with editors, editorial boards, mailing addresses and such pertinent information as statements of scope, sponsoring societies, and advertising and subscription rates. Instructions to contributors are reprinted in their entirety—including information on the number of manuscript copies required, desired format, correct style for typing footnotes and references, rules for the preparation of charts, tables and graphs, and more.

"For rapid access, journals are arranged alphabetically by their National Library of Medicine abbreviations." Circulation figures for some titles are to be found in a table of journal characteristics, which also lists 73 journals adopting Vancouver style.

The appendixes include the uniform requirements for manuscripts, January 1979, also called Vancouver style or the uniform requirements. Also included are the Recommendations of the World Medical Association, guiding medical doctors in biomedical research involving human subjects, comprising the Declaration of Helsinki as revised in the Declaration of Tokyo. There follows a selected list of editorial reference guides, which includes detailed information on the list of journals indexed in *Index Medicus,* style manuals, and SI units.

Journals from the United States predominate in *Information to Authors, 1980-1981;* however, a selection of titles from the United Kingdom is included.

192. International Steering Committee of Medical Editors. "Uniform requirements for manuscripts submitted to biomedical journals: List of participating journals," *British medical journal,* 6206 (Jan. 5, 1980): 23. (At head of title: Style matters.) [Supplements in part *Information to authors, 1980-1981: Editorial guidelines reproduced from 246 medical journals. (see* item 191).]

Lists 89 journals adopting the Vancouver style previously cited in *Index Medicus* as of mid-December 1979.

Bibliographic style: "From January 1980 the new format for bibliographical references specified in the Vancouver style will appear in *Index Medicus,* the *Bibliography of Medical Reviews,* and *Abridged Index Medicus.*"

192a. Warner, Steven D., and Kathryn D. Schweer. *Author's guide to journals in nursing & related fields.* New York: Haworth Press [c1982] 219p. ([*Author's guide to journals series*]) ISBN 0-91772-11-9; LC card 82-1058; $24.95. Library of Congress catalogs under title.

More than 350 profiles of scholarly journals in nursing and related fields are provided. Each entry includes journal title, manuscript address, types of articles accepted, major subjects of interest to the journal's editors, topics preferred, inappropriate topics, review procedure, review period, manuscript word length, number of manuscript copies required, publication lag time, early publication option, acceptance rate, authorship restrictions, page charges, style requirements, style sheet, acceptance of revised theses and student papers, reprint policy, subscription address, annual subscription rate, frequency, circulation, affiliation, and where the journal is indexed/abstracted. There is an index of subjects, titles, and keywords.

Journals from Australia, Canada, India, Israel, Kenya, Netherlands, New Zealand, Nigeria, Philippines, Singapore, South Africa, Sweden, Switzerland, Thailand, United Kingdom, and United States, are included.

Non-English journals, most newsletters and minor state and local periodicals are excluded.

MUSIC

General Style

193. *Notes for contributors to the sixth [i.e. New Grove] edition of Grove's dictionary of music and musicians.* [London]: Macmillan, 1971. vii, Pamphlet (19p.) (Cover title: *Grove's dictionary: Notes for contributors.*)

Divided into 2 parts: general style and house style. The former deals with "Style and Approach, Article Structure and Content, Article Headings, Music Examples, Illustrations, Bibliographies, Lists of Works, Editions, Sources, [and] Cross-references." The latter section includes "Spelling, Hyphens, Punctuation, Quotation, Dates, Numbers, Italics, Capitals, [and] Languages." The "Notes" conclude with abbreviations for general use, instruments, titles of periodicals, reference books, and anthologies and collected editions.

Bibliographic style: "Footnotes are to be avoided." "Bibliographies of over 30 items should be classified, preferably as follows: A Catalogues, bibliographical items etc B Source material (documents, letters, the subject's own writings, iconography etc) C Biography, 'life and works', studies etc."

NEWSPAPERS AND NEWS MAGAZINES*

In the introduction to his *The Stylebook for Newswriting* (*see* item 195), Spencer Crump outlines the history of newspaper style manuals:

> Until the 1950s, every newspaper could economically have its own style because there were no technological reasons to make this impractical. After establishing its style, a newspaper could have its reporters follow it in their stories, and editors could direct copyreaders to edit wire copy for spelling, punctuation, capitalization, abbreviations, the use of figures or spelled numbers, and other "style" standards.
>
> The 1950s brought the application of computer technology to typesetting: now instead of only typing copy, wire service machines also produced punched tapes capable of operating typesetting machines. This technological advance resulted in the development of the AP-UPI [Associated Press-United Press International] joint stylebook; for this manual, the wire services agreed on basic style rules. In turn, most local newspapers adopted the book as their standard, and for the first time, style became virtually nationwide in a single form. Some newspapers, usually those with the larger circulations, continued to use their own stylebooks. . . .
>
> These "universal" stylebooks [i.e., AP and UPI] reached their most sophisticated form in 1977 when each wire service issued a bulky (more than 200 pages) stylebook. While not identical in all respects, they were basically the same. In addition to the traditional "style" entries, these guides included explanations of subjects about which journalists frequently report. They also provided tidbits of "almanac" information which, while helpful to newswriters, could hardly replace the many reference books so necessary to a journalist.
>
> The wire services' stylebooks were intended especially for AP or UPI personnel to use in gathering and transmitting copy for worldwide use. Because the stylebooks are readily available to newspapers and radio/TV outlets which need them, they are wisely used by non-wire services newswriters. These users must eliminate many rules and points which are relevant and applicable *only* when writing for a wire service.†

194. Associated Press. *The Associated Press stylebook and libel manual: With appendixes on photo captions, filing the wire.* Christopher W. French, Eileen Alt Powell, Howard Angione, eds. [Reading, MA: Addison-Wesley, 1982, c1980.] iv, 286p. ISBN 0-201-10091-6; LC card 80-51657. $7.95pbk. (Earlier edition 1977.) Bibliography: pp. 245–46.

---

*Because of the "dictionary arrangement" of style manuals for newspapers and news magazines, remarks on bibliographic style have been omitted from the following 7 items.
†Reprinted from Spencer Crump, *The Stylebook for Newswriting,* published by Trans-Anglo Publishing Co., 1979, p. 7, with permission from the author.

". . . we will review entries annually, making necessary changes by wire notes during the review period.

"Each new printing of the Stylebook will incorporate the changes that have been announced on the wires."

Dictionary arrangement of terms of interest to the editors and writers of the Associated Press. The stylebook is particularly thorough on religious organizations, geographic names, and governmental bodies. This manual complements those of Bobby Miller (*see* item 198) and Spencer Crump (*see* item 195).

195. Crump, Spencer. *The stylebook for newswriting: A manual for newspapers, magazines, and radio/TV.* Corona del Mar, CA: Trans-Anglo Publishing Co., [c1979]. 112p. ISBN 0-87046-052-8, ISBN 0-87046-051-Xpbk; LC card 79-2440. $7.95, $2.95pbk.

Contains an introduction on the history of newspaper style, and sections for the stylebook, copyreading symbols, and proofreading symbols.

"This stylebook is basically compatible with the Associated Press and United Press International stylebooks."

"This manual hopefully is *avant garde* in its presentation of style in that it was written to reflect what newspapers and stations are doing. The wire stylebooks lag somewhat in presenting changes since they are compiled for a large part on the basis of what has been done and changes require some time to reach the wire manuals."

"This guide, unlike the wire services' stylebooks, is intended primarily for the writer associated with a *local* newspaper, radio/TV news outlet or magazine." The stylebook (pp. 12–111) forms the bulk of the manual. Entries are arranged alphabetically and include abbreviations, acronyms, and common and proper nouns. Some terms, e.g., "capitalization," "military titles," and "quotation marks," are given considerable space.

An interesting and useful supplement to the style manuals of the Associated Press and United Press International.

196. Holley, Frederick S. *Los Angeles Times stylebook: A manual for writers, editors, journalists and students.* New York: New American Library, c1981. xi, 239p. ISBN 0-452-00552-3; LC card 80-28897. $6.95. ("A Meridian book.") Bibliography: pp. 238–39.

"This book is an adapted version of the style manual used by the writers and editors of the Los Angeles Times. Although the title identifies this book as a '*style*book,' it also deals with questions of usage. . . ." Geographical terms, grammatical usage, and proper nouns are listed in alphabetical order. "The Los Angeles Times Stylebook is designed to be used in conjunction with one primary reference source: Webster's New World Dictionary of the American Language, Second College Edition."

Very prescriptive in its interpretation of language use and grammatical rules. Lengthy discussions are to be found under: Asian names, capitalization, courtesy titles and sex references, headlines, punctuation, and religious references. An up-to-date newspaper style manual that is useful as a reference source if the above limitations are taken into account.

197. Jordan, Lewis. *The New York Times manual of style and usage: A desk book of guidelines for writers and editors.* [New and enl. ed.] [New York]: Quadrangle/New York Times Book Co., [c1976]. 231p. ISBN 0-8129-0578-4, ISBN 0-8129-6316-4pbk.; LC card 75-8306. $10.00, $5.95pbk. (Earlier edition 1962.)

The manual consists of a list of terms arranged alphabetically, included primarily for their spelling, capitalization, or abbreviation. Some words have no explanation, e.g., "debutante." Other words have a paragraph or longer explanation, e.g., "women," which has a 2-page commentary. Some geographic terms are out of date, e.g., "Territory of the Afars and Issas," now called Djibouti. There seems to be no consistency in which geographic terms were selected and which were ignored. In other cases, short essays, e.g., "fairness and impartiality," create a set of pronouncements otherwise interspersed with words the *Times'* editors considered important.

198. Miller, Bobby R. *The UPI stylebook: A handbook for writers and editors.* [New York]: United Press International, [c1977]. 196p. LC card 79-102216. $3.00. (Revision of the 1960 edition) Bibliography: p. 196.

"This new and enlarged edition of the UPI Stylebook does not undertake to be a manual of literary style. Its primary purpose is to achieve consistency in spelling, capitalization, punctuation and usage for newspaper wires."

An alphabetical arrangement of terms, the choice of which is tailored to meet the day-by-day needs of reporters and editors. Includes entries not readily available, e.g., time zones, weather, U.S. Court of Appeals. Although not as detailed on foreign names as Jordan (*see* item 197), the *UPI Stylebook* is better on sports in the United States. These 2 manuals complement each other very well.

199. Rose, Turner. *U.S. News & World Report stylebook for writers and editors.* Washington, DC: U.S. News & World Report, [1981, c1977]. xii, 237p. ISBN 0-89193-001-9; LC card 77-21337. $7.95. ("Third printing, revised, 1981.")

> The 17 chapters are: 1. style and content, 2. bias: avoid it, 3. abbreviations, 4. capitalization, 5. punctuation, 6. figures, 7. foreign currencies, 8. names of persons, 9. natives, nationals, 10. church and clergy, 11. weapons, planes, astronautics, 12. medical terms, 13. trademarks, 14. political regions of the U.S., 15. captions, charts, boxes, credits, 16. slang, dialect, jargon, and 17. compound words. The book includes an extensive combined index and word list.

> Very up-to-date presentation of contemporary news magazine style. It is well designed, and the large print is easy to read. The novel idea of combining the index with problem words lets the user know immediately if the *U.S. News & World Report Stylebook* will provide an answer to the question at hand. The approach to writing the news is comprehensive, and the volume well written. Problems are discussed at length, and reasons are presented for editorial judgments. Especially useful are the chapters on abbreviations; capitalization; church and clergy; names of persons; and natives, nationals; and the section on sexism. This stylebook supplements the newspaper style manuals, and in many cases provides a more detailed presentation of the style problems of writing the news than those of the press agencies in the United States.

200. Webb, Robert A. *The Washington Post deskbook on style.* New York: McGraw-Hill, [1978]. xv, 232p. ISBN 0-07-068397-2, ISBN 0-07-068398-0pbk.; LC card 77-22958. $8.95, $5.95pbk. Bibliography: pp. 220–23.

> Includes a preface by Howard Simons and 14 chapters: 1. standards and ethics, by Benjamin C. Bradlee, 2. newspaper law and fairness, by Christopher H. Little, 3. ombudsman: sauce for the gander, by Charles Seib, 4. taste and sensibilities, 5. good writing and correct usage, 6. abbreviations, 7. capitalization, 8. numerals, 9. punctuation, 10. spelling, 11. time elements, datelines, addresses, 12. deskwork: editing, headlines, bylines, captions, typography, 13. the federal government, and 14. local government. Indexed.

> Good on legal terms and local government in the District of Columbia, Maryland, and northern Virginia. Chapter 12 is well illustrated. The index is detailed, which is essential in a work not arranged alphabetically as most of the other newspaper style manuals are. Poor quality paper used in copy examined.

NONPRINT MATERIALS

General Style

201. Fleisher, Eugene B. *A style manual for citing microform and nonprint media.* Chicago: American Library Association, 1978. x, 66p. ISBN 0-8389-0268-5; LC card 78-9375. $4.50. Bibliography: pp. 65–66.

Divided into 3 parts: footnote and bibliographic citations for nonprint media, specific rules for elements of collation in the bibliographic citation, and sample footnote and bibliographic citations. Fleisher's manual covers the following nonbook materials: charts, dioramas, filmstrips, flash cards, games, globes, kits, maps, microforms, microscope slides, models, motion pictures, pictures, realia, slides, sound recordings, transparencies, and videorecordings.

Bibliographic style: simplified. The section on microforms is too short to be useful. Two titles providing additional information are the *Anglo-American cataloguing rules* (2nd ed.), and Alma M. Tillin and William J. Quinly's *Standards for cataloging nonprint materials: An interpretation and practical application* (*see* item 202).

202. Tillin, Alma M., and William J. Quinly. *Standards for cataloging nonprint materials: An interpretation and practical application.* 4th ed. Washington, DC: Association for Educational Communications and Technology, c1976. xiii, 230p. illus. ISBN 0-89240-000-5, 898; LC card 75-38605. $8.95. (Edition for 1968 by NEA's Department of Audiovisual Instruction has title: *Standards for cataloging, coding, and scheduling educational media;* rev. ed. 1971 by the Cataloging Committee of the Association for Educational Communications and Technology; 3rd ed. 1972 by the Information Science Committee of the Association for Educational Communications and Technology.) Bibliography: pp. 225–26.

"The terms *nonprint, nonbook,* and *audiovisual* are used interchangeably to designate all materials that are not in the traditional book format. The rules are not designed to cover manuscripts or music, nor ephemeral material such as newspaper clippings and illustrative material of various sorts which are of temporary value and do not merit full cataloging." The book is divided into 2 sections: cataloging rules, based on *Anglo-American cataloging rules, North American text: Chapter 6, Separately published monographs* (Chicago: American Library Association, 1974), and the cataloging rules as applied to specific media. For each type of material, sample cards illustrate cataloging that ranges from the fully descriptive to the very simplified.

Specifically covered are audiorecordings, charts, dioramas, filmstrips, flash cards, games, globes, kits, machine-readable data files, maps, microforms, models, motion pictures, realia, slides, transparencies, and videorecordings. Appendix 2 contains a glossary of nonbook terms. Indexed.

Valuable for examples and citations for material difficult to describe bibliographically.

PHYSICS

Journal Style

203. American Institute of Physics. Publication Board. *Style manual for guidance in the preparation of papers for journals published by the American Institute of Physics and its member societies.* 3rd ed. Prepared and edited by David Hathwell and A. W. Kenneth Metzner, under the direction of the AIP Publication Board. New York: American Institute of Physics, 1978. vii, 56p. illus. ISBN 0-88318-001-4; LC card 78-59836. $7.50. (''AIP Publ., R-283.'') (First ed. 1951; 2nd ed. 1959; rev. 1963, 1965, 1967, 1968, 1969, 1973.) Bibliography: pp. 53–54.

> Member societies are the American Physical Society, Optical Society of America, Acoustical Society of America, Society of Rheology, American Association of Physics Teachers, American Crystallographic Association, American Astronomical Society, American Association of Physicists in Medicine, and the American Vacuum Society.

> Divided into 5 parts: I. summary information for journal contributors, II. preparing a scientific paper for publication, III. general style, IV. mathematical expressions, and V. figures. The 12 appendixes are: A. statements of editorial policy for AIP and member-society journals, B. correct or preferred spellings of frequently occurring words, C. units of measure, D. standard abbreviations, E. alphabets available for typesetting, F. special symbols available for typesetting, G. journal title abbreviations [ca. 347], H. symbols used in correcting proof, I. physics and astronomy classification scheme, J. Physics Auxiliary Publication Service, K. copyright, and L. AIP Soviet translation journals. Indexed.

> Bibliographic style: no bibliographic style is presented, but the section on footnotes and references is well illustrated with various types of

citations. "In book references always include the title, the editor's name if any, the publisher's name and location, and the year of publication. In references to reports do not use abbreviations for the names of laboratories or agencies; spell them out."

Very useful for its presentation of mathematical expressions and illustrated material. Very detailed.

PSYCHOLOGY

General Style

204. American Psychological Association. *Publication manual.* 3rd ed. [Washington, DC: 1983, 208p. illus. ISBN 0-912704-57-8; LC card 83-2521. $15.00 [First edition published as v. 49, no. 4, pt. 2 (July 1952) of *Psychology bulletin;* 2nd ed. 1974].

> Divided into 7 chapters: 1. content and organization of a manuscript, 2. expression of ideas, 3. APA editorial style, 4. typing instructions and sample paper, 5. submitting the manuscript and proofreading, 6. journal program of the American Psychological Association, and 7. bibliography, which includes a history of the *Publication Manual.* There is an appendix on material other than journal articles, i.e., theses, dissertations, and student papers. Indexed.

> Bibliographic style: changes made in the 3rd edition include: "The year of publication is placed in parentheses immediately after the author's name. Reference notes have been eliminated; therefore, all references (except personal communications) are included in the list of references at the end of the article. In a reference to an article or a chapter in a book, inclusive page numbers of the article or chapter are given in parentheses immediately after the book title. The official two-letter U.S. Postal Service abbreviations for states (e.g., CA, not Calif.) are used in the reference list."

> *This manual is one of the major style manuals used in North America. It is followed not only by the writers of psychology articles, but also by many publishers of education journals and books. At least 112 journals follow APA style. The 3rd edition of the Publication Manual is considerably* enlarged from the 2nd edition. Heavy emphasis is placed on the publication of journal articles, and much of the manual is organized around this purpose. The manual is well designed and authoritative for anyone publishing in the fields of psychology and education.

205. Hollis, Joseph W., and Patsy A. Donn, eds. *Psychological report writing, theory and practice.* [2nd ed.] Muncie, IN: Accelerated Development, [1979]. xv, 296p. Forms. ISBN 0-915292-21-2; LC card 79-64499. $12.95pbk. Bibliography: pp. 277–81.

Divided into 5 parts: I. purposes, methods, and philosophy, II. confidentiality and security, III. writing style and errors, IV. outlines, samples, and forms, and V. manuscript writing. Indexed.

Bibliographic style: although the authors stress the use of the *Publication Manual of the American Psychological Association,* bibliographic citations presented on p. 274, item 7, and the Callis and Caruso items p. 277 do not conform to APA style found on p. 122 of the *Publication Manual of the American Psychological Association.*

Hollis and Donn discuss in depth the problems encountered in writing a psychology report, with prominent use of sample reports and psychological forms. For bibliographic use, the *Publication Manual of the American Psychological Association* is preferable.

Journal Style

206. British Psychological Society. Standing Committee on Publications. *Suggestions to contributors.* Leicester: [c1979]. 27p. ISBN 0-901715-08-5pbk. £2.00.

Divided into 4 parts: introduction, the general arrangement of articles, the preparation of the manuscript, and submitting the manuscript. Preparation of the manuscript includes title, abstract, headings, tables, footnotes to a table, tables from other sources, figures, graphs and illustrations, quotations, copyright arrangements, abbreviations, punctuation with abbreviations, numbers, statistics, mathematical copy, metrication, references, alphabetization in references, and address of author. The manual concludes with sections on submitting the manuscript, consisting of correcting and altering the manuscript, proofreading, proof correcting, returning the proofs, offprints, and copyright arrangements.

Bibliographic style: Harvard. Includes examples for unpublished articles, books, articles in books, and articles in periodicals.

The society issues 5 periodicals: *British Journal of Psychology, Journal of Occupational Psychology, British Journal of Medical Psychology, British Journal of Social and Clinical Psychology,* and the *British Journal of Mathematical and Statistical Psychology.*

207. Markle, Allan, and Roger C. Rinn. *Author's guide to journals in psychology, psychiatry & social work.* New York: Haworth Press, [c1977]. xvi, 256p. ([*Author's guide to journals series*].) ISBN 0-91724-00-3; LC card 76-50377. $19.95.

> The introduction includes abbreviations used for abstracting and indexing services, and style manuals. An alphabetical listing of journals, late entries, and an index by subject, title, and keyword are included.
>
> Each entry includes journal title, manuscript address, major content areas, articles usually accepted, topics preferred, inappropriate manuscripts, where the journal is indexed/abstracted, subscription address and cost, publication lag time, early publication option, review period, acceptance rate, style sheet, style requirements, circulation, and reprint policy.
>
> The guide includes approximately 463 English language journals and is a valuable reference work for authors, editors, and librarians.

RELIGION

General Style

208. Church of Jesus Christ of Latter-Day Saints. *Style guide for publications.* 2nd ed. Salt Lake City, UT: [1978]. 74p. in various paginations (loose-leaf) with 3 punched holes for a ring binder. $2.50. (First ed. 1972.) (Available only from the Church's Distribution Center, 1999 West 1700 South, Salt Lake City, UT 84104: stock number PBIC0008.) "Chapter 17 of the *Style Guide,* 'Books and Periodicals Frequently Quoted in Church Publications,' is printed separately (PXIC 0570) and is not included in this packet. It is intended primarily for editors in the Church Office Building."

> "The *Style Guide* is not intended as a comprehensive statement on all questions of style. Because Church publications generally follow the principles suggested in *A Manual of Style* (published by the University of Chicago Press and herein referred to as 'Chicago'), this guide is concerned primarily with matters in which Church style differs from that of Chicago or is more specific than Chicago's suggestions." It is divided into 18 topics that roughly match the first 18 chapters of the Chicago manual: style reference sources; manuscript preparation; usage; copyrights, permissions, and publishing information; punctuation; spelling and distinctive treatment of words; capitalization; num-

bers; scripts; quotations; charts; forms; proper use of Latter-Day Saint titles; abbreviations; source citations, cross-references, and footnotes; bibliographies; and scouting terminology. The index is excellent.

Bibliographic style: generally follows the style as represented in *The Chicago Manual of Style*. Parentheses are omitted and months of the year are abbreviated. Descriptive terms are frequently used to explain ambiguous titles, e.g., *The Law* [family home evening manual].

A very detailed manual with many examples that might be usefully employed as a supplement to *The Chicago Manual of Style*. Especially good on publishing information, capitalization, quotations, abbreviations, source citations, cross-references, and footnotes.

209. *Concordia stylebook: A guide for authors and editors.* [7th ed.] St. Louis, MO: Concordia Publishing House, [1975]. 35 leaves. (First and 2nd eds. 1960; 3rd ed. 1962; 4th ed. 1963; 5th ed. 1965; 6th ed. 1969.) Includes bibliographical references.

Divided into 11 sections: preparation of the manuscript, quotations, headings, footnotes, bibliographies, editing and designing, galley proofs, indexing, rules for the preparation of copy, hints to editors of periodicals and distinct editions of the *Lutheran Witness*, and proofreaders' marks.

Bibliographic style: identical to that presented in *The Chicago Manual of Style*, except for the use of roman numerals as volume numbers. Footnote style follows "the latest revision of the *MLA style sheet*."

Interesting treatment of Biblical material and religious works by the major Lutheran publishing house.

210. Pilgrim Press. *Style rules: The Pilgrim Press/United Church Press.* Rev. New York: [1977]. 56 leaves. Photocopy.

Divided into 11 chapters: manuscripts; references and sources; capitalization; punctuation; italicization; quotations; spelling, abbreviation, syllabification; numerals; Biblical material; bibliographies, footnotes, indexes; and nomenclature.

"*A Manual of Style* (12th ed.; Chicago: University of Chicago, 1969). This is generally regarded as 'the publisher's bible' and is to be used as the final authority in all printing and publishing matters not covered by the United Church Press style rules. . . ."

Bibliographic style: follows *The Chicago Manual of Style*. Only a few annotated examples are given.

Includes a nomenclature for the United Church of Christ. Other unique items are the list of capitalized and noncapitalized words (mostly religious), abbreviations for the books of the Bible, and a detailed chapter on Biblical citation.

211. Regular Baptist Press. *Regular Baptist Press stylebook: Capitalization, hyphenation, spelling [and] general office style.* [Schaumburg, IL: 1980?]. 33p.

Alphabetical arrangement of religious terms, many containing references to chapter and section in *The Chicago Manual of Style*. Following the alphabet are brief sections on forms of scripture citation, punctuation, and approved versions of the Bible.

Bibliographic style: no bibliographic style is presented.

212. Zondervan Publishing House. *The Zondervan manual of style for authors, editors, and proofreaders.* Grand Rapids, MI: [1977, c1976]. ISBN 0-310-3501-2. $3.50.

Contains 8 chapters: I. bookmaking, II. punctuation, III. spelling and special use of words, IV. numbers and abbreviations, V. capitalization, VI. proofreaders' marks, VII. proofreaders' sample, and VIII. reference works. No index is provided.

Bibliographic style: no examples shown, but follows *The Chicago Manual of Style*. "It [this manual] has been compiled by the editors and proofreaders in conjunction with *A Manual of Style* published by the University of Chicago Press, which is our accepted standard and a helpful addition to the library of every editor and author. . . .

"For most topics we have placed in parentheses the number of the section in the Chicago Manual (CMS) where additional information and examples can be found. However, this guide serves also as a supplement for those instances wherein our house style deviates from the above works or for those topics that need emphasis and special treatment because of the religious character of our materials."

Included is a short section on reference to scripture and a lengthy list of Biblical and religious terms.

SCIENCE

General Style

213. Australia. Commonwealth Scientific and Industrial Research Organization. Editorial and Publication Service. *CSIRO style guide.* East Melbourne, Victoria: 1977. 22p. illus. ISBN 0-643-00152-2. ["Reprinted 1977 (with amendments)."]

> A short guide to CSIRO style. "If you are submitting a paper to one of the Australian Journals of Scientific Research you should also read the 'Notice to Authors' published in the Journal itself." Paragraphs are devoted to materials and format, pagination, the length of the paper, spelling and punctuation, units, abbreviations, and symbols, footnotes, numbers, dates, trade names, and trade marks. Additional sections are devoted to the title, the author, the abstract, headings, tables, and the acknowledgments. Special attention, although brief, is given to mathematical, chemical, and biological papers. A "Selected Bibliography" includes books on general style, units, and nomenclature. Appendixes include a list of "Standard and Preferred Spellings," "International System of Units," and lists of "Abbreviations, Symbols and Conventions" and "Proof Readers' Marks."
>
> Bibliographic style: Harvard, with the date of publication the first element after the initials of the first and middle names. Titles are abbreviated and italicized. Other usage is unique and deserves study before being used.

214. Barrass, Robert. *Scientists must write: A guide to better writing for scientists, engineers and students.* New York: Wiley; London: Chapman and Hall, 1978. x, 176p. illus. ISBN 0-470-99388-X; LC card 77-18561. $9.95, £3.95. ("A Halstead Press book.") Bibliography: pp. 166–67.

> Divided into 14 chapters: 1. scientists must write, 2. personal records, 3. communications, 4. how scientists should write, 5. think—plan—write—revise, 6. thoughts into words, 7. using words, 8. helping the reader, 9. numbers contribute to precision, 10. illustrations contribute to clarity, 11. reading, 12. reports and theses, 13. preparing a report on an investigation, and 14. talking about science. Indexed.
>
> Bibliographic style: for books, the surname is followed by initials of first and middle names, date in parentheses may follow, title is underlined, edition, number of volumes in bold face type, but not "vol." There follow name of the place, name of the publisher, the year of publication, and pagination. For articles in journals, the order

of names is the same as for books; there follow the title of the article and the name of the journal underlined, the volume number in bold face type, the issue number in parentheses, the date of issue, and inclusive pagination. Abbreviations are taken from the *World List of Scientific Periodicals*. Titles are not abbreviated in research and development reports. No examples are provided.

The use of standards in the section on the "List of References" brings up their use throughout this guide. Barrass notes the role that standards play in the writing of a scientific paper. He lists international standards and standards of the United Kingdom and the United States. Unfortunately, the most recent one cited is 1975, leaving the manual somewhat out of date. Users of this guide should carefully consult the indexes to the standards for later information.

"This book, by a scientist, is not a textbook for English grammar. Nor is it just one more book on how to write a technical report, or a thesis, or a paper for publication. It is about all the ways in which writing is important to students and working scientists and engineers in helping them to remember, to observe, to think, to plan, to organize, and to communicate."

A readable manual. Its use of standards is a laudable and welcome innovation.

215. Blackwell Scientific Publications. *Recommendations for authors.* [London: 197–?.] 7p.

Divided into 10 parts; general, headings, permissions, references, tables, illustrations, proofs, index, preparation of new editions, and some common abbreviations.

Bibliographic style: modified form of Harvard style with dates in parentheses. "The journal title should be abbreviated according to the *World List of Scientific Periodicals,* or the full journal title may be used."

"Useful further information can be found in the series *Cambridge Authors' and Printers' Guides.* Among the titles are *Preparation of Manuscripts and Correction of Proofs, Making an Index, Notes and References, Punctuation,* and *Prelims and End-Pages.*" (*see* items 99–100)

216. Booth, Vernon H. *Writing a scientific paper and speaking at scientific meetings.* 5th ed. London: Biochemical Society by permission of Koch-Light Laboratories [Colchester: Biochemical Society Book Depot, distributor], 1981. 48p. £2.50, $6.00 U.S. (First edition 1971 by Koch-Light Laboratories; 2nd edition between 1971 and 1975 issued privately by the Department of Biochemistry, University of Cambridge; 3rd edition 1975 "published in *Biochemical Society Transactions* 3, 1–26"; 4th edition 1977.) Bibliography: pp. 33–36.

Divided into 68 unnumbered sections: glossary of some printers' terms; explanation—examples; before you write; when to begin writing; arrangement of a scientific paper; where to start; stocktaking; title & key words; summary; introduction to a paper; materials & methods; results; discussion & conclusion; references, bibliography or literature cited; literary style—clear English, incomprehensible sentences, noun adjectives, wrongly attached participle, pudder, 'make every word count', pronouns, hedging; tense, mood & voice; choice of words— plain words, foreign words, elegant variation, homonyms; conveyance of ideas without element of doubt; cosmetics; good workmanship endures; language in flux; revision of the script must not be hurried; spelling; stops or punctuation , ; : .—a new paragraph, colons, semicolons, the comma, dashes, the hyphen, parentheses, the solidus, initial letters; abbrevns & cntrctns; headings or captions— make your headings work; tables; are all your numbers correct?; illustrations; numbering of figures, tables & references during their preparation; units & quantities—numbers & ratios, paradox; apparatus, materials & writing techniques; alterations & corrections; preparing the typescript—split words, balloons, cover sheet, additions, the typewriter's type face; drawing the diagrams for reproduction; journey's end for the script; preparation of a doctoral dissertation or thesis; good sense; emotion & modesty in scientific writing; and addressed to writers for whom English is a second or foreign language. The section "Further reading" is an annotated bibliography. The remainder of the booklet is taken up with information on speaking at scientific meetings. An index is introduced with this edition.

Bibliographic style: no bibliography style is presented.

This booklet is a commentary on the specifics of writing and publishing rather than a prescriptive set of instructions. Booth's essay offers good advice and it is easy to read.

217. Day, Robert A. *How to write and publish a scientific paper.* Philadelphia, PA: ISI Press, [c1979]. xi, 160p. illus. ISBN 0-89494-008-8, ISBN 0-89495-006-1pbk.; LC card 79-12467. $15.00, $8.95pbk. Bibliography: pp. 153–54.

Divided into 26 chapters: 1. what is a scientific paper? 2. how to prepare the title, 3. how to list the authors, 4. how to list the addresses, 5. how to prepare the abstract, 6. how to write the introduction, 7. how to write the materials and methods section, 8. how to write the results,

9. how to write the discussion, 10. how to cite the acknowledgments, 11. how to prepare the literature cited, 12. how to design effective tables, 13. how to prepare effective illustrations, 14. how to type the manuscript, 15. where and how to submit the manuscript, 16. the review press (how to deal with editors), 17. the publishing process (how to deal with printers), 18. how to order and use reprints, 19. how to write a review paper, 20. how to write a conference paper, 21. how to write a thesis, 22. ethics, rights, and permissions, 23. use and misuse, 24. avoiding jargon, 25. how and when to use abbreviations, and 26. a personalized summary. The 6 appendixes are: 1. list of journal title word abbreviations, 2. abbreviations that may be used without definition in table headings, 3. common errors in style and in spelling, 4. words and expressions to avoid, 5. prefixes and abbreviations for SI units, and 6. accepted abbreviations and symbols. Indexed.

Bibliographic style: 3 reference styles are briefly examined: 1. "name and year," also called Harvard style, which has been "very popular for many years and is still used in many journals, although that system is not as widely used as it once was" (a good critique of this style follows), 2. "citation order system," which "is simply a system of citing the references (by number) in the order that they appear in the paper," and 3. "alphabet-number system" where the citation is "by number from an alphabetic list of references." Day notes that the third system seems to be gaining more and more appeal (p. 40). The *American National Standard for Bibliographic References* is not mentioned in the manual or its references. In particular, writers in the fields of biology and chemistry should consult the manuals of their disciplines before choosing one of the above styles.

A manual of short essays, each of which is devoted to a particular problem or topic. Succinct, but effective writing makes Day's manual useful for anyone wishing to brush up on a problem. Only a few examples are included.

218. *A guide for preparing manuscripts [for] authors, editors, reviewers, [and] staff personnel.* Rev. ed. Prepared by a committee convened by the Printing and Publishing Office, National Academy of Sciences; National Academy of Engineering; Institute of Medicine; [and] National Research Council. Washington, DC: National Academy of Sciences, 1975. v, 60p.

Divided into "Parts of a Manuscript" and "Preparation of Manuscript Copy." The former deals with the cover and front matter, the text, references, notes, and bibliographies and back matter. The latter part covers style, including spelling and compounding of words, capitalization, punctuation, italics, abbreviations, and numbers. Treatment of tabular and graphic material is well presented, and is followed by a section on special problems such as mathematics, symbols, units, nomenclature, permissions, and symposia. The second part of the manual concludes with "Instructions to Typists Preparing Manuscripts." Unmarked appendixes cover the Greek alphabet, proofreading marks, and other suggested style guides. The index is well done.

Bibliographic style: out of date for the sciences.

A well-thought-through manual that needs revision. More information is needed on the requirements of the individual sponsors of the guide.

219. Royal Society of London. *General notes on the preparation of scientific papers.* [3rd ed.] London: 1974. 31p. ISBN 0-85403-065-4; £0.50. (First ed. 1950; 2nd ed. 1965.) Bibliography: pp. 19–28.

Divided into 10 parts: 1. the typescript, 2. title and headings, 3. abstracts, 4. numerical results, 5. references, 6. tables, 7. illustrations, 8. nomenclature, units, symbols, and abbreviations, and sources for anatomy, atomic energy and nuclear science, biochemistry, biology, botany, chemistry, crystallography, engineering, geography, geology, mathematics, medical science, microbiology, mineralogy, physics, physiology, statistics, and zoology, 9. dictionaries and books on writing, and 10. proof correction.

Bibliographic style: Harvard, with abbreviations of journal titles in accordance with the *World List of Scientific Periodicals* (1963) and subsequent supplements. Volume numbers are in bold-face type.

Valuable for its lists of sources for nomenclature, including British standards, for the sciences cited above. Needs to be brought up to date.

220. Trelease, Sam F. *How to write scientific and technical papers.* Cambridge, MA: M.I.T. Press, [1969, c1958]. xii, 185p. ISBN 0-262-70004-2pbk.; LC card 58-6803. $4.95. Bibliography: pp. 177–80.

Divided into 7 chapters: 1. the research problem, 2. writing the paper, 3. good form and usage, 4. tables, 5. illustrations, 6. publication review, and 7. proofreading.

"The present volume is an outgrowth of two earlier books: 'Preparation of Scientific and Technical Papers' (three editions, Copyright 1925, 1927, 1936), and 'The Scientific Paper, How to prepare it, How to write it' (two editions, Copyright, 1947, 1951)."

Bibliographic style: 2 styles are presented: 1. Harvard style, called "text reference to citation" by Trelease and 2. "footnote citations," where footnotes are numbered consecutively by superscripts in the text with the complete citation is at the end of the chapter.

"This manual is intended to meet the practical needs of students and research workers who are preparing illustrated papers or reports on scientific or technical subjects." The Committee of Biology Editors in the third edition of the *CBE Style Manual* (1972) note: "A profound, but concise, treatment of the logical considerations in scientific writing. Highly recommended as the most scientific of the many books on this subject."

SOCIAL SCIENCES

General Style

221. Mullins, Carolyn J. *A guide to writing and publishing in the social and behavioral sciences.* New York; London: Wiley-Interscience, [c1977]. xvi, 431p. ISBN 0-471-62420-9, ISBN 0-471-02708-1pbk.; LC card 77-1153. $15.95pbk. Bibliography: pp. 411–17.

Divided into 4 major parts: I. outlines, first drafts, revisions, and resources, II. authors, articles, and scholarly journals, III. general instructions for preparing a book manuscript: monographs, textbooks, and edited collections, and IV. publishers, prospectuses, and contracts: the forthcoming book. The 4 appendixes are: A. journals: exclusions and supplements, B. suggestions for class papers, dissertations, proposals for research grants, progress reports, and oral presentations, C. a sample prospectus for a monograph, and D. a guide for typists. The short index is inadequate for such a long, detailed work.

Bibliographic style: under a horizontal table entitled: "Characteristics of Journals in the Social and Behavioral Sciences," is an in-depth discussion and comparison of the styles in *The Chicago Manual of Style* (item 113) (both the humanities and the scientific sections), the American Psychological Association Manual (item 204), the American Sociological Association Manual, the *Journal of American Statistical Association*, the Modern Language Association *Style sheet*, 2nd ed. (later ed.: item 165), the *Sage Journal*, and Turabian (item 94). Some 540 titles of journals are listed with the style used for the years 1973–75. Sample pages of bibliographies are given. The discussion of documentation may be of interest to editors.

This guide exhaustively treats publishing in the social sciences. Unfortunately, the text is presented in short broken paragraphs that destroy the continuity of the prose style and turn what is otherwise an excellent reference book into a style manual that is as difficult for the editor to use as it is for the student.

222. Skeldon, Grania. *Style manual.* Boroko, Papua New Guinea: Institute of Applied Social and Economic Research, 1979. 105p. K2, or $3.00 U.S.

Divided into 15 chapters: 1. abbreviations, 2. capitals, 3. dates, 4. headings and subheadings, 5. indirect speech, 6. numbers, 7. proofcorrecting, 8. quotations, 9. references, 10. "Scholarship: A Single Notion," by Mary-Claire van Leunen, 11. spelling, 12. tables, 13. words and expressions commonly misused, 14. other aspects of bad style, and 15. miscellaneous, which includes the set order for the names of the nation's provinces. Appendix 1 describes how to write a curriculum vitae. The index is detailed.

Bibliographic style: Harvard.

"This *Style manual* was originally intended for the use of researchers at the Papua New Guinea Institute of Applied Social and Economic Research. The aim was to help them to write up their material in a way which would be acceptable in international academic circles and to raise the general standard of publications issued by the Institute. I also wished to establish a IASER house style."

"The basic source of materials contained in the manual consists of internal directives issued by the United Nations to its editorial staff between the years 1967 and 1973." Other sources include Kate L. Turabian's *A Manual for Writers of Term Papers, Theses and Dissertations* (*see* item 94) and *Student's Guide for Writing College Papers* (*see* item 95), Brooke Crutchley's *Preparation of Manuscripts and Correction of Proofs* (*see* item 99, no. 2), and other style manuals.

A prescriptive manual that is easy to use because of its layout and its detailed index. Particularly interesting as it varies from style manuals from both Australia and New Zealand.

Journal Style

223. Linton, Marigold. *A simplified style manual: For the preparation of journal articles in psychology, social sciences, education, and literature.*

With the assistance of Bonnie Faddis Trafton. New York: Appleton-Century-Crofts, [1972]. xix, 184p. ISBN 0-13-810135-3; LC card 72-79609. Out of print. Bibliography: p. 175.

Divided into 10 chapters: 0. style, 1. title, 2. by-line (authorship), 3. abstract, 4. introduction, 5. method, 6. results, 7. discussion, 8. references, and 9. article. The appendixes cover the metric system, abbreviations, spelling, references on style, and proofreader's marks. Indexed.

Bibliographic style: American Psychological Association as represented in its *Publication Manual* (1967) [now replaced by the third edition (1983)].

"Although this manual has been shaped by a legion of sources, it is based primarily upon the recommendations of the 1967 Revision of the *Publication Manual of the American Psychological Association.* . . . The APA recommendations have been expanded or annotated to include comment on current journal practice. My primary source for current practices was the *Journal of Experimental Psychology* and most of the examples reflect usage of recent issues in that journal."

This manual has not been updated by the information in the second or third editions of *Publication Manual of the American Psychological Association.* The material included in the manual does not reach the aspirations contained in the title. Writers in the social sciences, education, and literature would do better to use the better-known manuals. This discursive manual is difficult to use as a reference book.

SOCIOLOGY

Journal Style

224. National Association of Social Workers. *Information on NASW professional journals.* [Washington, DC: 1979.] 15p. ISBN 0-87101-100-X. Bibliography: pp. 12–14.

Divided into 4 parts: 1. NASW publications policies and procedures, 2. procedures for submission and review of a manuscript, 3. annotated reference list on writing and style, and 4. responsibilities, structure, and function of the NASW publications program. Includes guidelines for submitting papers to *Health & Social Work, Practice Digest, Social Work, Social Work in Education,* and *Social Work Research & Abstracts.*

Bibliographic style: no bibliographic style is presented. Only footnote style is discussed with a few examples.

225. Sussman, Marvin B. *Author's guide to journals in sociology & related fields.* New York: Haworth Press, [1978]. xv, 214p. (*Author's guide to journals series.*) ISBN 0-917724-03-8; LC card 78-1952. $16.95.

The introduction is followed by a table of abbreviations from abstracting and indexing services and style manuals. A short list of style manual publishers is included. The core of the bibliography is a listing of approximately 350 journals arranged alphabetically by title. Journals included come predominantly from the United States. However, titles from Australia, Canada, India, Ireland, and the United Kingdom are cited also.

Each entry contains journal title, manuscript address, type of articles accepted, major content areas, topics preferred, inappropriate topics, number of manuscript copies, review period, publication lag time, early publication option, acceptance rate, authorship restrictions, subscription address, annual subscription rate, where the journal is indexed/abstracted, circulation, page charges, style requirements, style sheet, revised theses, student papers, reprint policy, and frequency. Indexed by subjects, titles, and keywords. Journals selected for inclusion are taken from "those English-language journals included in *Sociological Abstracts,* and journals listed under the heading of 'Sociology' in the 1976 Edition of *Ulrich's International Periodicals Directory.*"

A good first place to start for authors in search of a publisher. As there is no style manual for sociological publications, individual titles would have to be examined for the particulars of style.

ZOOLOGY

General Style

226. Australia. Commonwealth Scientific and Industrial Research Organization. *Preparation of zoological papers with special reference to taxonomy.* [Melbourne]: 1977. 5p. ISBN 0-643-00269-3.

"These recommendations deal with zoological papers in the following fields: (a) general, (b) faunistic, biogeographical and ecological, and (c) taxonomic. They should be considered in conjunction with the 'CSIRO Style Guide' available also from the Organization" (*see* item 213).

Appendix I. Disabled People

227. ''Avoiding handicapped stereotypes: Guidelines for writers, editors and book reviewers,'' *Interracial books for children bulletin,* v. 8, no. 6/7 (1977): 9.

> ''The guidelines . . . were prepared by the Center on Human Policy, the Center for Independent Living in Berkeley, Disabled in Action of Metropolitan New York and the Council on Interracial Books for Children.''

Most of the above issue of *Interracial Books for Children Bulletin* is devoted to counteracting the stereotypes of disabled people.

228. McGraw-Hill Book Co. *Guidelines for fair representation of disabled people in McGraw-Hill Book Company publications.* [New York?: between 1978 and 1981.] [5]p. ISBN 0-07-04529-3.

> ''The major goal of this report is to alert editors and authors to the need for fair representation in Book Company publications for the 36 million citizens of the United States who may have a handicap or disability. Our concern is twofold. First, McGraw-Hill educational and reference materials should avoid offending disabled or handicapped people either by the use of stereotypes or by omission. Second, these publications should raise the consciousness of the balance of the population so that they can appreciate the dignity and worth of all their fellow human beings.''

> ''All three terms—exceptional, handicapped, and disabled—are in use and acceptable. McGraw-Hill does not advocate one over the others. For purposes of this document, however, the term 'disabled people' has been selected. This term should be understood as synonymous with 'handicapped people' or 'exceptional persons.' ''

In addition, the guidelines review other sources for a discussion of the background and the problem of terminology.

Appendix II. Nonsexist Language

229. American Psychological Association. "Guidelines for nonsexist language in APA journals." Washington: 1977. 8p. (Publication manual change sheet, 2 for *Publication manual*, 2nd ed.)

> Divided into 2 parts: I. problems of designation and II. problems of evaluation. Each section is divided into 3 columns: 1. examples of common usage, 2. consider meaning; an alternative may be better, and 3. comment. No index is provided.

> Easy to read and authoritative.

230. McGraw-Hill Book Co. *Guidelines for equal treatment of the sexes in McGraw-Hill Book Company publications*. [New York?: 197–?] 16p.

> Divided into 4 parts: 1. the roles of women and men, 2. portrayals: human terms, 3. language considerations, and 4. parallel treatment. No index is provided.

> The format of this short pamphlet is to lay out the offensive term on the left, headed "no," with the nonoffensive term on the right, headed "yes." Easy to use because of its generous spacing and the tabular format.

231. Miller, Casey, and Kate Swift. *The handbook of nonsexist writing*. New York: Lippincott & Crowell, [1980]. ix, 134p. ISBN 0-690-01882-7; LC card 79-26851. $8.95. (Reprinted as a paperback by Barnes and Noble in 1981, ISBN 0-06-463542-2. $3.95.) "Reference notes": pp. 123–27.

> British edition: *The handbook of non-sexist writing for writers, editors and speakers*, revised by Stephanie Dowrick. London: Women's Press, 1981. ISBN 0-7043-3878-5pbk. £3.25.

> Divided into 6 chapters: 1. *Man* as a false generic, 2. the pronoun problem, 3. generalizations, 4. seeing women and girls as people, 5. parallel treatment, and 6. a few more words. The index is detailed.

"Our aim throughout has been to provide practical suggestions to speakers and writers already committed to equality as well as clarity in style, though in the process we tried to show why an apparently innocuous word or phrase may be injurious."

The detailed index makes this handbook an excellent source for nonsexist usage in the English language.

Index